D1124604

CHRISTINA STEAD

Women Writers

General Editors: *Eva Figes* and *Adele King*

Published titles:

Charlotte Brontë, Pauline Nestor
Fanny Burney, Judy Simons
Sylvia Plath, Susan Bassnett
Jean Rhys, Carol Rumens
Christina Stead, Diana Brydon

Forthcoming:

Margaret Atwood, Barbara Rigney
Jane Austen, Meenakshi Mukherjee
Anne Brontë, Elizabeth Langland
Willa Cather, Susie Thomas
Emily Dickinson, Joan Kirkby
George Eliot, Kristin Brady
Mrs Gaskell, Jane Spencer
Katherine Mansfield, Diane DeBell
Muriel Spark, Judith Sproxton
Edith Wharton, Katherine Joslin-Jeske
Women in Romanticism: Dorothy Wordsworth, Mary Wollstonecraft and Mary Shelley, Meena Alexander

Further titles are in preparation

Women Writers

Christina Stead

Diana Brydon

BARNES & NOBLE BOOKS
TOTOWA, NEW JERSEY

First published in the USA 1987 by
BARNES & NOBLE BOOKS
81 ADAMS DRIVE
TOTOWA, NEW JERSEY 07512

ISBN 0–389–20689–X
ISBN 0–389–20690–3 (Pbk)

Printed in Hong Kong

Library of Congress Cataloging-in-Publication Data
Brydon, Diana.
Christina Stead.
(Women writers)
Bibliography: p.
Includes index.
1. Stead, Christina, 1902–   —Criticism and
interpretation. I. Title.   II. Series.
PR9619.3.S75Z57   1987   823   86–22307
ISBN 0–389–20689–X
ISBN 0–389–20690–3 (pbk.)

Contents

Acknowledgements   vii

Editors' Preface   viii

1 A Waker and Dreamer   1

2 Redrawing the Boundaries   16

3 Finding a Voice   32
  Seven Poor Men of Sydney: Releasing new voices   32
  The Salzburg Tales: Ventriloquist's tricks   44

4 Parisian Affairs   48
  The Beauties and Furies: Becalmed off Cythera   48
  House of All Nations: The bank as whorehouse   58

5 Autobiographical Fiction   69
  The Man Who Loved Children: Celebrating the
    unhappy family   69
  For Love Alone: The voyage to Cythera   80

6 American Dreams   90
  Letty Fox: Her Luck: Beyond Cythera   90
  A Little Tea, a Little Chat: The whirligig of values   101
  The People with the Dogs: The communal dream   107
  Puzzleheaded girls   115

7 In the Hall of Mirrors   127
  Cotters' England: Humbug and humblepie   128
  The Little Hotel: Running from doomsday   138
  Miss Herbert (The Suburban Wife): Unawakened
    Venus   145

8 Stead and her Critics   159

Notes   174
Bibliography   180
Index   186

Acknowledgements

I am grateful to the University of British Columbia for a Humanities and Social Sciences Research Grant enabling me to begin research for this project in 1983–84 and for granting me sabbatical leave. The Social Sciences and Humanities Research Council of Canada provided a Leave Grant in the academic year 1984–85 that freed my time to write and enabled me to travel to Australia to consult the Christina Stead papers in the Australian National Library. Mrs Pam Ray, the Manuscript Librarian, and her staff were extremely helpful during the week I spent there. Professor R. G. Geering, Stead's literary executor, has kindly allowed me permission to quote from the manuscripts. He has also been most helpful in making extensive comments on early drafts of my first fiive chapters. My colleagues, Sherrill E. Grace and Catherine LeGrand, also provided helpful responses to early drafts of the first chapters. All errors, of course, remain my own responsibility. My greatest debt remains to Bill Brydon for his patience and willingness to renounce his own time on the computer so I could wrestle with my ideas about Stead, a writer who has interested me since I began my Ph.D. thesis at the Australian National University in 1973 on Australia's expatriate novelists. A Commonwealth Scholarship first took me to Australia and acquainted me with Stead's fiction.

Editors' Preface

The study of women's writing has been long neglected by a male critical establishment both in academic circles and beyond. As a result, many women writers have either been unfairly neglected or have been marginalised in some way, so that their true influence and importance has been ignored. Other women writers have been accepted by male critics and academics, but on terms which seem, to many women readers of this generation, to be false or simplistic. In the past the internal conflicts involved in being a woman in a male-dominated society have been largely ignored by readers of both sexes, and this has affected our reading of women's work. The time has come for a serious reassessment of women's writing in the light of what we understand today.

This series is designed to help in that reassessment.

All the books are written by women because we believe that men's understanding of feminist critique is only, at best, partial. And besides, men have held the floor quite long enough.

EVA FIGES
ADELE KING

1 A Waker and Dreamer

'I write what I see', claimed Christina Stead. And what she saw was special. Fiercely independent and fiercely loyal in her private life, she went her own way without regard to literary fashion. The key to this woman of many apparent contradictions lies in her belief in integrity, her sense that she was a born 'word-stringer' whose function in life was to record with honesty what she saw and heard in the world around her.[1] Insisting that she wrote out of instinct and would continue to write on a desert island if her only materials were her fingers and the sand, she nonetheless worked hard at revising her writing to sharpen the vision that shaped her work.

That vision was essentially egalitarian. Not only men and women but the rich and poor were also entitled to equal consideration in her eyes. She would allow no means of dividing human beings from one another to diminish her respect for the humanity of each. No character is beneath her attention. Each decision a character makes, however, defines where that person stands in relation to life. As in Shaw's moral universe, the central choice that divides the characters in Stead's fiction is that between the life-affirming and the life-denying. Stead recasts this choice as one between embracing love and all that entails, specifically creativity and interaction with others, or selling out one's deepest desires in return for some share in what Stead terms the amenities.

Stead's central metaphor for life is the voyage of

discovery. Two images from her childhood fixed the
fictional patterns that voyaging might take. A horrifying
picture from the Sydney Art Gallery – 'The Sons of
Clovis' – created an indelible impression on her mind that in
later years she associated with the penalties to be paid for
loyalty. In this painting, the sons, hamstrung by their
enemies, drift helplessly down a river. Stead recalled her
emotions: 'Tied. Hamstrung. They can't move. I don't
know why, but that got me.'[2] Immobility, the inability to
act independently, seems to have been her greatest fear.
This nightmare voyage is countered by a fusion in Stead's
mind of Darwin's purposeful voyage of scientific discovery,
as narrated by her father, and her reading of the wily
Ulysses' wandering through his island-studded world.
Their motivated voyages, not the drifting of the sons of
Clovis, became models for her own. But the image that
seems most to have fascinated Stead was embodied in
another painting – 'The Embarkation for Cythera' by the
French eighteenth-century painter Watteau. Here men and
women, at various stages in their wooing, prepare together
to embark on a voyage towards the mythical island of love,
Cythera.

At several points in her fiction, Stead characterised the
passionate creativity and subversive force of true love as a
voyage to Cythera. Her fictional characters divide themselves
between those who embark on the voyage and those who
refuse the voyage to remain on the shore. Stead's fiction
invites her readers to embark on a similar voyage beyond
the dull shores of the conventional into the uncharted
waters of others' lives and the unexplored possibilities of
alternative ways of seeing. For her, this had to be a
communal enterprise, with men and women joining forces
to seek a better life together.

People are increasingly turning to Stead's fiction for a
number of reasons. Australians are building a national
culture in which her work holds a significant place. Women

are looking to her and other women writers to help make sense of their experiences. Christina Stead presents a hard-headed treatment of an often misunderstood topic – human love. She writes of love from a woman's perspective, but as few women have written of love before. In her honesty and her curiosity she may still be ahead of her times. The current interest in Bakhtin's theories about the polyphonic novel have encouraged those interested in twentieth-century fiction to revalue Stead's multi-voiced texts for the original experiments they are. Although no writer is ever completely original, Stead's work fits few preconceived patterns. We are only beginning to learn how to read her fiction because it challenges many of the assumptions we have been trained to bring with us when we pick up a novel.

Her originality derives more from the unusual circumstances of her life than from any deliberate attempt to shock. Her life spanned most of the twentieth century and three continents, beginning and ending in Australia after years in England, Europe and the United States. The dynamic metaphor of life as a voyage of discovery characterised her life as well as her fiction.

This is the first study of Stead to consider how Stead's status as a woman affected her fiction and the first to focus on those elements of her writing that are most immediately relevant to women. Stead saw herself as a writer. She resented being ghettoised as a woman writer. She herself did not judge people by gender but by their actions. Nonetheless, she lived in a society that did discriminate against women and she recorded its workings in her fiction. Many of Stead's challenges to conventional thinking about the ways in which fiction constructs our view of life become more understandable when viewed from a feminist perspective.

Her recent death in March 1983 makes this an appropriate time to reassess her achievement: an impressive list of eleven novels and two collections of short stories. This

chapter's title applies Stead's assessment of her father to
her own life and work.[3] Like him she was 'a waker and
dreamer', intensely alive to things as they are yet capable of
dreaming how they might be otherwise. Equally drawn by
the psychological and spiritual worlds revealed through
dreams as by the material worlds studied in the waking
hours by the scientist and economist, she sought to combine
the perspectives of wakers and dreamers alike in her
writing. She mixed imagery taken from her favourite
English romantic poet, Shelley, praising the perceptions
afforded by dream, with contemporary Marxist imagery of
waking to the dawning of a new age. Both the dreaming
and the waking were essential to her vision of the complete
person, male or female.

Born female in 1902, she wrote in a period when to write
as a woman was automatically to work at a disadvantage.
Refusing to accept her gender as a handicap, she
compounded this problem of reception by writing as if
unaware that she should find this circumstance a liability.
Her work never fitted conventional ideas of how a woman
should write but neither does it fit entirely comfortably
with currently popular streams of feminist fiction. A born
iconoclast, Stead distrusted all orthodoxies.

She probably owed at least some of this maverick
originality to her Australian origins and to her remarkable
father, who impressed on her the importance of seeing life
through scientific eyes rather than through the filters
manufactured by romance or religion. Stead's birth in 1902
came a year after the birth of Australia as an independent
nation. She grew up unhampered by many Old World
cultural restrictions, with a sense that a new and better
world could be created in Australia. Pointing out that
women received the vote early there, she says it never
occurred to her to feel inferior to men.[4] She did, however,
feel different from most of the people she knew, both men
and women. Whereas they seemed satisfied with what they

had, she was propelled by dreams, inspired by her reading of Goethe's life, to seek a world of greater intellectual and creative activity – the life she finally found with her husband, the economist and writer William Blake.

Their roaming life together nurtured her remarkable creative output but did nothing to help her critical reception, for in this as in everything else she defied academic pigeonholing. She wrote about Australia, America, England and France with an insider's ear and eye. This very versatility denied her a home in any single national tradition. Only recently has Australia come of age sufficiently to claim her along with its other expatriate writers. Now, with the growth of the new field of 'women's writing' and the reissuing of all her books in paperback, Stead is beginning to find the audience she deserves.

The second generation of her family to be born in Australia, Christina Ellen Stead was born in Sydney in July 1902 to David Stead, a well-known marine biologist, and his wife Ellen (née Butters). When Stead was two and a half her mother died. She retained no memories of her. When she was four and a half her father remarried. His new wife produced six children. As the eldest child, Stead received much of her father's attention, particularly in her early years. She told an interviewer that in effect she was 'the eldest son', in whom her father invested many of his hopes.[5] When the other children came, however, she had to combine this role with the new one of second mother, helping to raise and care for the growing family. Of her stepmother Stead said she 'was kind to me until her first child was born, and then I was the outsider'.[6]

Her father, a man of considerable accomplishment and integrity, exercised great influence over the thinking of his first-born child. Much of Stead's independence of mind may come from his early encouragement. Both Stead's grandfathers were freethinkers (the term then for atheists) although both grandmothers were religious. Stead's parents were agnostic. Stead grew up with science taking the place of conventional religion. While her father worked on his first book, *Fishes of Australia*, which appeared in 1906, she memorised the Latin names of fishes. Her father told bedtime stories of the geography of the land, conveying his passion for its mysteries to his children. They grew up with a menagerie of wild animals kept in the stables of their large old house. As she grew older, Stead herself took on her father's role of inventing bedtime stories for the others, while helping her stepmother with the endless household chores. Her stepmother's unwilling subjugation to the tyranny of childbirth impressed on her at an early age the importance of controlling woman's biological functions if she is to find freedom. Stead had her fill of women's traditional role of caring for house and children in her childhood. Reading could provide escape but only writing promised control over an environment that seemed bent on controlling her. Stead translated the magic and the tyrannies of this period of her life into her greatest novel, *The Man Who Loved Children*.

When Stead's father lost his job through a refusal to compromise his principles, the family experienced several years of acute poverty. Stead, by this time in her twenties, was his only confidante. Her experience of poverty during this period sensitised her to the roles money plays in determining values in a capitalist system. A posthumously published autobiographical story. 'The Old School', takes this subject as its explicit theme, but all her work is informed by her recognition of the importance of material conditions for understanding human relations.

Her own experiences were supplemented by her voracious reading. As a young girl, she discovered Shakespeare, reading him through from beginning to end once a year. She admired Webster, idolised Shelley and 'fell overboard for Balzac' after she learned to read French in high school.[7] Her lifelong devotion to French, a subject prohibited by

her puritanical father, may have been the first overt sign of
her own stubborn independence – inherited from him and
sometimes, naturally, turned against him. But she read all
her father's books too: Darwin and popular Australian
works by Henry Lawson, Banjo Paterson and Steele Rudd.
Much Australian literature explores social injustice and
since the big gold rushes of the mid-nineteenth century
questions the wisdom of founding social ethics on the
artificial valuing of gold. Here she would have found
further confirmation for her suspicion of authority and its
arbitrary linking to the mythology of gold. And here too
she would have encountered savagely misogynist fictional
worlds where women were marginalised or ignored, often
denied even the limiting roles of love object or nurturer
assigned them in European fiction.

Originally her father wanted her to become a scientist
like him but as his growing family made increasing
demands on his financial resources he encouraged her to
leave school early and profit from her facility with language
to earn money for the family as a journalist. Although she
rejected this suggestion, believing she did not yet know
enough to write for a living, this family pressure influenced
her decision to attend Teachers' College instead of university
(for which she had won a scholarship) in 1920. After a two-
year training course she worked as a Demonstrator in
Experimental Psychology at the College in 1922, taught the
next year, but found it too much of a strain on her voice,
so in 1924 did psychological testing in the schools.
Continuing to find teaching a nervous strain, she studied
typing and shorthand at night school, until she could leave
the Education Department to work as a secretary. For the
next four years she contributed to the support of her family
while saving what money she could to give herself what she
fancifully thought of as her own travelling fellowship to
Europe.

These years of stubborn saving towards a goal few of her

contemporaries could understand are recorded in her novel
For Love Alone. Stead was 26 when she finally sailed away
in search of her destiny, acutely aware that she must seem
a failure in the eyes of those for whom early marriage was
the only suitable goal for a young woman like her. Stead
mentions in interviews that her father disapproved of
novels. How interesting that his daughter should have
become a novelist! Yet her father also took her first
manuscripts to the Australian publisher Angus & Robertson,
explaining that this story writing 'seems to be really the
only thing . . . that Peg is thoroughly interested in'.[8]
(Stead was called Peg by her family and close school
friends.) These stories were rejected. Although Robertson
found them 'remarkable for their language and imagery',
he could not imagine a sufficient Australian audience for
such 'poetical fantasies'. He recommended approaching an
English publisher but nothing more seems to have been
done with these stories, which were later lost in a French
hotel room.

Arriving in London in May 1928, Stead found a job with
Strauss and Company, grain exchange merchants. William
Blake, the man who hired her, later became her husband.
Blake was already married, although separated from his
wife, who was reluctant to divorce him. Consequently, he
and Stead lived together until they were finally able to
marry in 1952.

Blake, eight years older than Stead, had grown up in the
United States, the child of German Jewish immigrants. He
had begun work on Wall Street at the age of fourteen,
working his way up to become editor of the *Magazine of
Wall Street* in New York before coming to work as the
Managing Director of the London Scottish Banking
Corporation in London in 1928, when he met Stead. In
addition to his financial work, he wrote romantic and
historical novels and read learned books in French and
German for British and American publishers. In the preface

to his best-known book, *Elements of Marxian Economic Theory and its Criticism: An American Looks at Karl Marx*, Blake explains: 'My title to speak of Marxian political economy comes from the world of economic practice. For thirty years a statistician, economist, financial editor, banker, and grain merchant, I have found the study of political economy in my evenings a running commentary on the employment of the day'.[9] Gregarious while Stead tended to be a loner, talkative while she preferred to listen, financially capable while she disliked thinking about money – Blake was the ideal partner for Stead. They complemented one another. He was to support her, financially and emotionally, for 40 years.

That winter, before they knew each other well, Stead struggled against sickness, brought on by her single-minded determination to meet her goals, and wrote her first novel, *Seven Poor Men of Sydney*, thinking that if she died she would leave something behind her. The next year, after they both had moved to Paris to work in a new bank owned by Strauss and Company in the Rue de la Paix, Blake discovered the manuscript. He sent it on his own initiative to the publisher Peter Davies, who agreed to publish it if she wrote him another book first. Stead had just returned from the Mozart Festival in Salzburg. She hastily wrote *The Salzburg Tales* and both books appeared in 1934.

The following years were productive for Stead. She attended the first international Congress of Writers for the Defence of Culture (a Popular Front Congress) in Paris in 1935 and wrote an account of her impressions in 'The Writers Take Sides', arguing that 'the disruption of the bourgeois world, its disorders and anomalies, the frightful insistence of economic questions leaves the writer, whatever his origin, quite at sea'.[10] While some writers might have found such uncertainty unnerving, Stead welcomed the chance to rethink inherited certainties. Paradoxically, she

was most at home when 'at sea'. The sea voyage remained
her metaphor for the questing spirit that for her defined
our humanity. She had entitled an article on the short story
'Ocean of Story', an unpublished autobiographical fragment
'A Fish in the Ocean of Story' and would portray her
autobiographical heroine Teresa in *For Love Alone* as an
Australian Ulysses,[11] characteristically casting her female
hero in the active role of the quester, traditionally reserved
for the male. As these metaphors show, Stead was interested
in social questions but her interest lay in the human
repercussions of politics rather than in their abstract
analysis.

The Beauties and Furies appeared in 1936 and her first
major novel, *The House of All Nations*, in 1938. An ambitious
account of Europe between the wars, this panoramic novel
of greed and betrayal dramatises the tendencies in Western
civilisation that were leading it toward fascism in the
between-the-wars period. Stead revels in the revealing
details of human interactions. Like Jean Rhys, another
expatriate from the colonies, she anatomises the financial
and psychological entanglements of love in Paris during the
1930s. But more firmly than Rhys, she places these personal
involvements within the larger context of social structures.
Both writers question the complicity of victims in their
victimisation, but the victim is never central in Stead's
fictional worlds. Her Paris is not the seedy Paris of losers
immortalised by Rhys.

Neither is Stead's Paris the city popularised by the
American writers of the 'lost generation', created during
the boom years of the 1920s. Nor is it the paradise of
adolescent American male fantasies depicted by Henry
Miller in later years. Stead dissects the myth of Paris as the
city of lovers and expatriates in *The Beauties and Furies*,
showing that the liberation it appears to offer is a trap, and
a trap that is built on the oppression of local women in
particular. In *The House of All Nations* she extends the

portrait, to show that the real business of Paris – as the centre of European capital – is money-making. Both novels delight in the variety and extravagance of this metropolitan centre, while questioning the necessity of their foundations in oppression.

The Man Who Loved Children, generally regarded as her best book, moves on to demolish her society's most cherished myth, that of the family. This 'celebration of unhappy family life', as Stead herself characterised it, appeared in 1940.[12] The timing could hardly have been worse. During the Second World War, a novel about an unhappy middle-class family could not have seemed of urgent interest. Although it received favourable reviews at the time, it soon went out of print. Now, in the United States at least, it is her best-known novel.

The House of All Nations had been based on Stead's experiences working in the bank in Paris. *The Man Who Loved Children* records her early family life growing up in Sydney, but transferred to a Washington location 'in order to shield the family'.[13] In Louisa Pollit, Stead portrays genius as an adolescent girl, translating the pressures of puberty and an unhappy family life into a torrent of words: stories for her younger brothers and sister, a tragedy for her father, a sonnet sequence for her teacher. In Louisa's father Sam, 'the man who loved children', she dramatises all the liberal forces the child must escape if she is to realise her genius: the benign paternalism in effect as repressive as outright tyranny, the self-satisfied egotism, the sentimentality bordering on fascism. *For Love Alone*, published in 1944, takes up the autobiographical account where *Children* left off, to show its heroine, with a different name and background, making her own way in the world after leaving her family. It is Stead's most hopeful book, claiming that a determined spirit can break through some of the bonds restraining creativity to challenge the common sense that insists fulfilment is not possible.

Stead and her husband spent the war years, from 1937 to 1946, in the United States, mostly in New York where she worked on the left-wing journal *New Masses* and lectured on the novel for a term at New York University. A brief period working in 1943 for MGM (Metro-Goldwyn-Mayer) in Hollywood as a Senior Writer ended when she was blacklisted as a result of the political persecutions of the McCarthy era. The influence of this new American environment and a shifting away from autobiographical experience mark the works of the next decade. *Letty Fox: Her Luck* (1946), *A Little Tea, a Little Chat* (1948), *The People with the Dogs* (1952) and *The Puzzleheaded Girl* (1967) all reflect back on this period, recording the impact of the Cold War on the lives of ordinary Americans. These books show how new economic conditions forced a revising of every version of the multifaceted American dream: of the inevitable rightness of love and marriage; of every man's search for a 'dream girl' and a fortune, by whatever means; of the nineteenth-century utopian dream of establishing communal retreats from commerce; of 'sowing wild oats' in Europe.

At the end of the war Stead and Blake returned to Europe. From 1946 to 1953 they lived a roving life, moving from one European city to another. In 1953 they decided to settle in London because Stead was fearful of losing her English. Stead's last great novel appears to owe its existence to this decision. Published in the United States under the publisher's misleading title *Dark Places of the Heart* in 1966 and in London under her own title *Cotters' England* in 1967, this is Stead's most powerful account of the human potential for creativity warped and wasted through a poverty so pervasive its victims have come to embrace it. It initiates the final phase of Stead's 'human comedy', dissecting the follies of post-war England as Balzac did those of nineteenth-century France.

It took Stead a long time to recover from her husband's

death from cancer in 1968. The two novels published before her own death in 1983, *The Little Hotel* in 1975 and *Miss Herbert (The Suburban Wife)* in 1976, although begun earlier, record an increasingly pessimistic view of people's capacity for creative change. Nonetheless it was during these years she first began to receive the attention that was long due her achievements. As late as 1968 she was recommended for but then denied the Britannica Australia Award on the grounds that her long expatriation disqualified her from full identity as an Australian. This scandal was remedied the following year when Stead accepted an invitation to visit Australia as a Fellow in the Creative Arts at the Australian National University in Canberra. In 1974 she became the first recipient of the Patrick White Prize and returned to Australia to live. In 1982 Stead was awarded the New South Wales Premier's Literary Award for her oustanding contribution to Australian Literature and in the same year she was elected an Honorary member of the American Academy and Institute of Arts and Letters. Her citation asserts that she had been 'long recognised as a novelist of world range whose many works combine social realism with unique imaginative power' and that she was 'truly a master of human comedy'.

Stead took her Australian identity for granted, just as she did her identity as a woman. Both shaped her, determined her experiences and to a large extent how she saw the world, but she saw no reason to fuss about the supposed disadvantages of either position. Curiosity, not the 'cultural cringe' (Australians' internalisation of the European belief that the colonies were inferior), first led her to travel to Europe. Circumstances – her marriage to Blake – kept her there. She said: 'I feel about women's rights the same as I do about any human rights. I suppose it's a natural extension of socialism: why shouldn't everyone have their fair slice of the pie?'[14] All her fiction insists on this larger social context; no character can be understood without reference to it. This sensitivity to context is her greatest contribution, not only to the tradition of women's literature but to literature in general.

Her novels stress culture over nature, showing how education plays a greater role than biology in shaping the images of women allowable under patriarchal capitalism. By dramatising the double binds this artificial situation uses to oppress women, her fiction demonstrates the supreme importance of consciousness – of how we see the world – to what we can do within it. While the majority of her women characters fail to attain the freedom they seek, each retains her integrity as a more complex human being than the conventional stereotypes would allow. Those who do win through to self-definition find that personal liberation lies in refusing to accept society's confusion of gender (socially constructed, culturally learned difference) with sex (biological difference). But for Stead, no one can become truly free until we have challenged all of the interlocking forms of oppressive domination on which our present system feeds.

Her interest in social and political alternatives to Western capitalism and particularly in human rights never deserted her. During the 1950s she acted as Secretary of the Australia – New Zealand Civil Liberties Society. Her curiosity about socialism in Cuba under Castro, in Chile under Allende and in Albania led her to join British friendship societies associated with these governments. Her manuscripts suggest she was working on a novel about 'tourists of the revolution' in Albania. Although this project never came to fruition, her indignation about American and Australian involvement in the Vietnam War led her to write a rare piece of commentary, focusing on the efforts of the North Vietnamese to reorganise their society's medical services more equitably in the face of devastating bombardment from the enemy.[15] For her, writing was never a retreat from life but an engagement with it – an extension of an involvement she lived as well as evoked in the books she wrote.

In *Parallel Lives* Phyllis Rose suggests that every marriage can be seen as a narrative construct whose fictional patterns in a writer's case are likely to conform to those which animate the writing.[16] I argue here that the voyage to Cythera as a shared voyage of discovery was the animating myth behind Stead's life and work. She saw sexual and creative fulfilment as inseparable and she believed they could only result from relationships of absolute equality. In her marriage, each respected the other's work. Each followed an individual path. After Blake's death, Stead explained: 'Our writing didn't affect each other but of course our interrelationship did. It's taken me all this time, five years, to get over his death, because there's a fabric, a structure, you see, built up between each other.'[17] When that disappeared, she had to begin again, like someone who didn't know anything. The shared vision was shattered.

Stead's insistence on cooperation between the sexes cannot please those feminists who believe women have given too much and men too little for too long. She had a horror of lesbianism and even of groups of women together that she attributed tentatively to the fact that she never knew her mother. She herself saw this antipathy as a weakness. But she also managed to maintain her independence within a long-lasting marriage during a period when such a relationship was rare. She brought to her marriage a commitment to living her life as a voyage of discovery. For all their differences, Blake shared that vision. She translated their experiences together into fiction remarkable for its questioning of socially indoctrinated gender differences. In her refusal to simplify, she provided women with few potential role models. Instead, she provided a vision of the world in which her readers could see clearly the consequences of the choices before them.

2 Redrawing the Boundaries

Other books devoted to Stead's writing – by R. G. Geering and Joan Lidoff[1] – are general introductions to her fiction as a whole. This study builds on their pioneering work to demonstrate how an explicitly feminist reading, through narrowing the focus, can reveal dimensions overlooked, too quickly skimmed over or misunderstood by the wider scan. Feminist criticism begins by making two related assumptions about literary experience: that women writers write out of an experience and perception of experience different to men's (whether that difference is biologically or socially inscribed is a separate and much more debatable question) and that women readers and critics may bring different expectations and perceptions to their reading than do men. From this position feminist criticism redraws the boundaries established by the male criticism we used to accept (on its own valuation) as 'universal': boundaries between what is and what is not literature, between what constitutes a well-made and what a poorly-made work of art, between what is and what is not 'realistic', and between what is and is not an acceptable literary subject. Stead's fiction challenges most of the assumptions pre-feminist criticism brought to literature. Feminist criticism can help us understand and value these innovations – even when it cannot fully account for them in terms of female experience alone.

Stead herself doubted whether a specifically female aesthetic existed, although she was prepared to entertain the possibility. She rejected the efforts of American feminists in the 1970s to identify a female aesthetic with a separatist lesbian consciousness, however. The search for those kinds of identifications is not helpful in understanding her work. Current feminist interest in mother–daughter relationships and metaphors of childbirth in art are similarly of little help in understanding the dynamics of Stead's art – unless one were to consider the significance of their lack of centrality in her work. Although Stead depicts childbirth scenes in her fiction (in *The Man Who Loved Children* and *Letty Fox*) as well as showing characters deciding to have abortions (Elvira Western and Letty Fox) these incidents are given no special emphasis in her work to mark their inclusion as intentionally revolutionary. Similarly, lesbianism and incest are treated as ordinary aspects of life despite the fact that when Stead was writing these subjects were still considered taboo. She seldom treats the mother–daughter relation in any depth and never valorises it. When her writing focuses on women's lives at all – and much of it does not – she documents the double lives lived by career women, trying to make a living while establishing or maintaining relationships with men. But generally speaking Stead's subject is never women at all but women and men in a variety of social relations.

The metaphors that do animate Stead's art tend to fall into three categories: firstly, physical imagery of hunger and eating, frustration and fulfilment and ambiguous imagery from the natural world with specific links to female sexuality: sea, moon, blood – these have the potential to enslave and liberate; secondly, imagery of the ideological webs that entrap the individual, made concrete in the hall of mirrors, the mysterious room without internal locks and the character who sells out his or her own interests in return for some share in the amenities; and finally, imagery of escape from these entangling webs: positively, through seafaring, wandering, walking – above all, embarking on the voyage to Cythera – and negatively, through madness or amnesia.

These three patterns of imagery shape Stead's fictional vision and reflect her perception of the patterns of oppression dominant in her experience of various Western societies throughout this century. In Stead's fiction gender, ideology and fictional form are closely related.

It is important to remember, however, that Stead's concerns in writing were never explicitly feminist. She believed the theories of the women's movement oversimplified the many relationships possible between individual men and women in practice. Immensely complex, these were ultimately not open to analysis along the lines of gender difference alone.

In the debate between 'radical feminists' and 'abstract socialists', lucidly described by Juliet Mitchell in *Woman's Estate*, Stead's intellectual position was closest to that voiced by the socialists. While recognising that women were oppressed, she did not believe that their shared oppression could transcend traditional economic class barriers to make them a separate class in their own right nor that an analysis of their oppression could succeed if divorced from its historical context. This position made her sound crotchety and impatient in her interviews, especially when she felt she was being invited to wallow in self-pity for the eternal sorrows of womankind. Her novels, however, combine the sophisticated analysis of the socialist position with the ability to capture the lived experience of oppression prized by the radical feminists. Her fiction creates a powerfully subversive vision that brings understanding and feeling together while insisting that there are no easy answers to the dilemmas it makes us see.

Both chronologically and temperamentally, Stead belonged to the period identified by Elaine Showalter as 'the Female phase, ongoing since 1920',[2] in which women writers rejected both imitation and protest in order to write from their own female experience as a source in itself of an autonomous art. Unlike Woolf and Richardson, however, whom Showalter identifies as the chief representatives of this period, Stead focuses less on the workings of human consciousness in itself than she does on the ironic contradictions between what her characters say and what they do, between how they see themselves and how we and others see them. Hers is an outward rather than inward-oriented art – a voyage out rather than a voyage in.

Stead made an extensive study of all Virginia Woolf's writing, noting with distaste the anti-Semitism of *The Years*, Woolf's English ethnocentrism and the ahistorical attitude that enabled her to live through four wars while barely making mention of them in her work. But it was the narrowing of Woolf's sympathies by class privilege that irked Stead the most. She notes: 'For she saw with less understanding than the most conservative and enraged suffragettes of her day. They thought only of the middle class women; she narrowed the women's movement for liberty, equality, fraternity down to "the daughters of educated men." '[3] Stead's own sympathies were much broader and her thinking about women's oppression much more thoroughly grounded in a materialist analysis. She saw that to blame the male sex as a whole was merely to reverse the sexist thinking that was used to keep women in an inferior place. For her the enemy was not individual men but the networks of power that structured all human relations. Any feminist study of Stead, then, must recognise her affinity with the tendency of contemporary English feminist theory to combine feminism and socialism in contrast to the American tendency to separate them.

Stead linked the two by making power her chief subject. Her novels show how power manifests itself through money or through love (through evading or embarking on the voyage to Cythera) and through the institutions that have arisen to accommodate these drives. Stead recognised the exclusion of women from institutionalised access to power, deplored it as unjust, but refused to sentimentalise its effects. Her satire mocks any character, male or female, who presumes to claim that men and women may be characterised by their sex/gender alone, whether that claim is made to denigrate or to celebrate women. Instead of attacking women's exclusion from male preserves of power directly, Stead preferred to attack it indirectly, through a display of how women's natural will to power adapts itself to this exclusion, finding other means to assert dominion over others or turning back against the self. To her, men and women shared a common human nature, driven by an almost biological, blind will to survive. She refused all mythologies that would present women as being closer to Nature, more carnal or more spiritual than men, mythologies that unconsciously accept the male as the standard from which woman becomes the deviation. For Stead, 'male' and 'female' were distinctions that provided little insight into character as such. Although she recognised that society had seized on biological differences to create further learned differences through education that could influence character development, she did not see these differences as conclusive. Despite the biological and social constrictions on women's freedom, she believed they must assume responsibility for their own lives as she herself had. While she saw that current ideologies and the social structures they legitimate worked more often to distort a woman's sense of selfhood than they did a man's, she remained convinced that obstacles could be overcome by an act of will. Nietszche's philosophy in particular appears to have influenced her thinking about the will to power in us all.

Stead's subject is power; Stead's style is dialectical. It is built on the acceptance of contradiction, of conflict and of struggle. It does not seek synthesis but clarification. It does not value the equilibrium of an order that has achieved stasis, seeing that ideal as a kind of death. Instead, she celebrates life as movement, disorder, passionate intensity renewing itself through release. Debates rage through the pages of all her work. Argument, discussion or conversation follow public meetings, lectures, even sermons, to form the substance of her fictional worlds. Monologue is never allowed sway for long; even her first person narratives show the narrator arguing with herself and recording the speeches of others. A multitude of released voices speak through the currents her fictions set in motion. In place of the orthodox forward movement of narrative that tells a story, Stead's is a fiction of interruptions. Untold stories challenge the dominance of a single narrative line. Silenced voices demand their turn at speech. Talk becomes more fascinating than story – talk for the sake of talk itself, but also because for Stead no real thought can occur without the give and take of ideas in debate.

Women's writing has often been seen as an act of aggression. To write at all, as Gilbert and Gubar suggest in their influential *The Madwoman in the Attic*, 'a woman writer must examine, assimilate, and transcend the extreme images of "angel" and "monster" which male authors have generated for her'.[4] This task involves most women writers in distinctive patterns of theme and imagery which identify a female literary tradition in English writing. Stead's work participates in this tradition, characterised by 'images of enclosure and escape, fantasies in which maddened doubles functioned as asocial surrogates for docile selves, metaphors of physical discomfort manifested in frozen landscapes and fiery interiors . . . along with obsessive depictions of diseases like anorexia, agoraphobia, and claustrophobia'.[5] Notes in the collection of her papers in the Australian National Library in Canberra show that she was well read in this tradition. But this tradition represents only one side of her work. Stead pairs these gothic themes with the kind of political and social acuity of observation we associate more often with a writer like Balzac.

This pairing leads to some serious modifications of the female gothic tradition. Stead herself seems never to have seen her writing as an aggressive act and never to have felt the need to 'kill the angel in the house'. Instead of examining traditional female roles and rewriting them, her work appropriates traditional male roles for her female characters without formulating that act as transgressive. Similarly, she casts male characters in traditionally female roles as a matter of course. In *For Love Alone*, Teresa casts herself as the valiant knight courting Jonathan Crow, who assumes the position of the 'belle dame sans merci', withholding love from his ardent suitor. Similarly, Letty Fox mourns her failure to keep her 'homme fatale', the elusively seductive Luke.

Joan Lidoff argues that Stead adapts the motifs of the traditional 'female gothic' to shape them into an original subgenre Lidoff labels the 'domestic gothic'.[6] Lidoff's phrase seems to be a response to one of the generating tensions in Stead's work: the pull between her scientist's eye for detail that tends towards a realism so exact it often seems a kind of hyperrealism on the one hand, and on the other her fascination with excess, with deviations of any kind from established norms of behaviour. In other words, Stead's style combines the gothic and the realistic in unusual ways. But there is nothing domestic about Stead's style or her subject matter. Stead spent most of her life in hotel rooms and cafés, and wrote about family politics to challenge conventional distinctions between the domestic and the public, not to uphold them. In Stead's fictional worlds there is no 'domestic' life separate from the social and political lives of a nation – they are part of a continuum in which each level reflects the others.

Beside the bank, the school, the business and political spheres, Stead places the comparable institutions of marriage – the relationship of husband to wife – and of the family – both the nuclear family formed by a marriage with children and the extended family of relatives. How individuals relate through institutional structures, how they survive or fail to survive, how they manipulate, deceive and share – this is her real subject. Stead's style allows each participant a voice, even the supposedly inanimate natural world – as in Michael's surrealistic excursion into the Australian countryside in *Seven Poor Men* – and even the features of the man-made urban world – as in Oliver's escapade at the Somnambulists' Club in *The Beauties and Furies*. Although Lidoff suggests that such fluid boundaries between animate and inanimate may be traced to traditional psychology's identification of women's 'weak ego boundaries', Stead's redrawing of boundaries here as elsewhere is a self-consciously political act, not an expression of a psychological tendency peculiar to women. Precisely because she is strong in herself she can challenge the boundaries traditionally drawn between her interests and the interests of others. Her fiction crosses boundaries because she *can* distinguish between self and other and not because she confuses the two. These gothic landscapes of enclosure and escape, of obsessive urges and extreme physical discomfort are not presented as fantasies in Stead's fiction but as the reality of everyone's everyday experience when seen from within. The seemingly surrealistic moments when the unconscious speaks are always grounded in the mundane – in the tasks of preparing food and washing up, of getting to and from work and of dealing with demands from family and friends. Stead's style thrives on the debate between unconscious and conscious impulses within the individual and on the political interactions between individuals at every level of experience, while stressing the internal contradictions of any attempt at synthesis.

In her first novel, *Seven Poor Men of Sydney*, Baruch Mendelssohn, the character modelled on her husband Blake, provides some insight into the generating principles of Stead's art. He points out that 'official drama is so fearfully unsatisfactory because of its big gross themes. Everyone knows it doesn't represent their own feelings at all. There would be a row if real situations were reproduced; it would undermine the State. The State is built on grotesque comic-opera conventions which no one dares mock at'.[7] Stead's realism sets out to create its own conventions, that will enable her art to reveal realities obscured by the official art that has preceded her and to mock the fake. Coming of age in the 1920s, she focused attention on ordinary people who toil in poverty and whose struggles to achieve some form of self-expression end in defeat. As the ensuing Depression yielded to prewar anxiety and then to postwar prosperity, she turned to the problems of middle-class women and men juggling the pressures of work and family. Whatever she portrayed reflected and contributed to the prevailing ethos of its own time. In her last published book, *Miss Herbert*, she mocks the trite eulogising of the 'universal' in literature for the obscurantist nonsense it is. Only in specifics can the truths that reside beneath the official clichés be seen.

She always insisted that she only wrote what she saw and what she heard. Hers is a profoundly sensuous art, relying on the author's own relation to the world through the medium of her senses, and depicting her characters as motivated by similar relations. As Don Anderson points out, Stead writes a drama of the appetites.[8] She makes us feel the hunger and cold of poverty, the pleasures and anguish of love, first of all. But because such sensations never occur in a vacuum, she also makes us see, more clearly than analysis ever could, how these sensations result from a complex of economic relations.

In her realism Stead saw herself as the objective scientist her father wished her to be, but turning her scientist's eye away from the cells that bored her, toward the study of human nature, the life assumed by those cells in their highest form of development. She is remarkably successful in creating an illusion of objectivity, perhaps because, in her writing at least, she appears to be non-judgemental, capable of recording the most monstrous behaviour with no sign of revulsion. Profoundly sceptical of all claims to authority, she balances every statement recorded with a counterstatement that carries equal weight. Her writing exudes a strong abhorrence of injustice, inequality, hypocrisy, lies and above all, illogic. She is always asking why and how such offences could be. Yet balancing such moral indignation she feels a fascination with decadence, with suffering, with deviance of all kinds, including madness. Her strong sense of community spirit is matched by an equally strong sense of individuality. She clearly delights in the exception to every rule. And her suspicion of cant inevitably includes idealism. The war between these opposites charges her work with powerful currents. In her more autobiographical writing, hope for the future appears to win a slight edge, but in her other books, cynicism threatens to swallow everything else. Always it is the tensions that keep the writing living. When they disappear, as they seem to at times in *A Little Tea, a Little Chat* and *The People with the Dogs*, the writing suffers.

Because her father was 'a great Darwinian', she read and 'enjoyed immensely' both *Origin of Species* and *The Voyage of the Beagle*.[9] But she never made the Spencerian mistake of translating Darwin's theories of the adaptation of species into the crude sociobiology of 'survival of the fittest'. On occasion, most memorably in *The House of All Nations*, she juxtaposes images of predators themselves becoming prey in the natural world against human predators in the social world; but never to suggest that this 'grab and graft' is the inevitable, natural order of things – only that we have made it so today. At times, Stead seems to be leaning toward determinism but she always pulls back from endorsing fatality to insist upon our ultimate freedom of choice. She resists all her interviewer's attempts, for example, to blame the family for adult problems. In her words, 'children grow up anyway . . . on the whole, people are pretty hard to twist'.[10]

Although none of her comments reveal an explicitly feminist critique of Freud, such as women are beginning to develop now, Stead rejected his theories as too rigidly determined to encompass her sense of the diversity and flexibility of human behaviour. She believed his middle-class position and his exclusive work with people his society termed abnormal prevented him from understanding the psychology of the majority of human beings. Rejecting Freud as 'old-fashioned' and doctrinaire, she preferred to rely on her own observations for creating what she called her 'drama of the person'. She told Raskin: 'The start of a story is like a love affair, exactly. It's like a stone hitting you. You can't argue with it. I wait and wait for the drama to develop. I watch the characters and the situation move and I don't interfere. I'm patient. I'm lying low. I wait and wait for the drama to display itself.'[11] The inspiration begins with the characters, whose relations with others slowly generate a story that Stead feels she is stalking rather than creating. Writing for her comes from watching others with patience, then shaping her words so their own dramas can emerge. Unlike conventional male ideas of writing as dominating a medium, imposing will on a fictional world, writing for her is an assisting into birth of a world of relations that clamours to be told. Naturally the fiction that results reflects her belief that each story demands its own shape and voice.

We recognise a Stead work primarily for the intensity of its focus on human relationships and for its refusal to draw boundaries where we would normally expect them. Stead's fiction provides insight into the roots of oppression in the twentieth century, showing that at base our problems derive from false distinctions between the interests of the self and of others, and that a solution may be found in imaginatively redrawing the boundaries.

Because the false distinction between the real interests of men and women as she sees them is demolished by love, love assumes a privileged place in her writing. Most of her work clears the ground, exposing all the sham attitudes that masquerade under the guise of love: romance, sentimentality, egotism, narcissism, fascism, racism, sexism. Stead shows how all these are allied in opposition to the passionate creativity and subversive force of true love, which for her is symbolised by the voyage to Cythera. Inspired by Baudelaire's poetic and Watteau's visual treatments of this theme of the journey to the island of love, Stead makes it her own through Teresa Hawkins' exclamation in *For Love Alone* that she always thinks of the voyage to Cythera as 'a Darwin's voyage of discovery'.[12] For Stead, love and creativity are synonymous. A woman who never had – and never wanted – a 'proper' home with fridge and car, she always said she found her home with her husband, and after his death, in her typewriter. For her, husband and typewriter were complementary – not antagonistic. The inspiration to write, like the impetus to love, began with people. Furthermore, Stead rejected the romantic and modernist elitism that would elevate the artist above ordinary human beings, believing instead, with the great Marxist theorist Antonio Gramsci, that all people were potentially creative.

Whereas a conventional thinker like *The Man Who Loved Children*'s Sam Pollit believes order must be used to resolve chaos, Stead argues through his daughter Louisa the Nietzschean contention that it is only from chaos – that is from a state of continual questioning rather than comfortable certainty – that one can give birth to 'a dancing star' – something new and beautiful in its dancing, in its refusal to be fixed. A conservative concern to keep everything in its place works to keep women and colonised countries down. Women who embrace such conservative views are acting against their own best interests, by denying themselves realisation through the chaotic experience of love, of an active engagement with the world. Stead never sees love in conventional romantic terms, either as surrender to another or as the conclusion to a story. For her it is always a power struggle – best unresolved – and always a beginning – an embarkation on another voyage of discovery. Stead's fiction puzzles over why anyone would acquiesce in her own oppression, choosing to remain on the dull shore of conventional compliance with authority. She contrasts the acquiescence of the sellout against the creative joy of the lover. All her writing acts to challenge orthodoxy either through a positive depiction of passion released or through negative dramatisations of passion repressed.

Critics looking for classical harmony in Stead, then, are bound to be disappointed. Although her books are much more carefully shaped than has yet been acknowledged, they do not always assume shapes familiar to conventional criticism's expectations. If she had been male and English, perhaps she would have been recognised sooner for the experimentalist she is. But if she had been male and English, she would probably never have made the experiments she makes, for all her books strike at the very roots of the idea of authority. In her life, Stead rejected the suggestion that she had made herself a literary career through her writing. Her Hollywood experiences no doubt encouraged her natural distaste for careerism, for putting money and personal advancement above the quest for truth. Writing was something she did, not for a living but because it made her feel good, in both senses of that word. By attuning her to her world, it took her beyond ordinary assessments of good and evil. She always sought to dissociate herself from the popular idea of the writer as someone special, set apart from the rest of humanity and pronouncing on it. Her writing depicts creativity as a natural human activity potentially open to all – even the downtrodden and ignorant like Joseph Baguenault of *Seven Poor Men*. She saw writing as an enabling and shaping act rather than an imposing of her own views on others. Her work forces her readers to think for themselves.

Feminist criticism has alerted us to the ways in which women writers have subverted the conventions of romance plots, by frustrating the traditionally coded expectations of a death or a wedding as the ending of a heroine's quest or by 'writing beyond the ending' to introduce a variety of alternative strategies. Although Stead uses few of the subversive strategies identified by Rachel Blau Du Plessis in her recent study, she writes 'beyond the ending' in her own fashion. Even when her novels seem to have traditional endings – the failure of the bank in *House of All Nations*, the weddings in *Letty Fox* and *The People with the Dogs*, death in *A Little Tea, a Little Chat* – they have been prepared for in such a way as to suggest their inability to end the forces set in motion by the texts in which they appear. For example, by the time Letty Fox has made the marriage that ends her story, marriage has been totally devalued as a goal and cancelled as an ending. Even Letty's alternative claim – that this wedding is her real beginning – fails to convince in the light of the context in which it has been presented. Here marriage is redefined as neither end nor beginning but merely another step – and possibly a self-defeating one – in Letty's struggle to get by.

In each of Stead's novels, the central character or more often, group of characters, give rise through their needs to the shape their stores will take. Sometimes she seems to go too far in her willingness to allow a character's context or a character's voice to override what we normally think of as plot, but the more fully one enters Stead's fictional worlds, the more such objections disappear as one begins to understand the complex patterns of alignment and the

dialectical relations she is seeking to illuminate. Stead's
fiction assumes unusual shapes and develops unexpected
rhythms – but always to convey the specific shape of a
particular experience. In her most memorable fiction, the
dominant element is usually a character – yet on closer
examination that character cannot be separated from the
particular web of relations in which he or she is entangled.
Sam and Henny Pollit, Teresa Hawkins and Jonathan
Crow, Nellie Cotter, Eleanor Herbert – are all inconceivable
without the worlds that make them comprehensible. As
Terry Sturm argues, 'The mode of realism she has invented
makes for inconclusiveness and open-endedness in her
novels, and an exploratory attitude towards character.'[13]
He points out that socialist realist critics find her writing
too individualistic while bourgeois realist critics find it too
dogmatic. No doubt some feminist critics would find it too
male-identified.

My intention here is to adapt Stead's own creative
approach as my critical one, allowing the novels themselves
to suggest the critical method best suited to understanding
them. The definition of realism they provide breaks down
the boundaries between public and private central to both
bourgeois and socialist realism and the boundaries between
the real needs of men and women sometimes thrown up by
contemporary feminist criticism. They break down these
boundaries by making apparent the tensions between
consciousness – the ways in which people perceive their
interests – and the actual material circumstances of their
lives. These ironies – sometimes comic, sometimes tragic –
create their own structures – sometimes of a classic
formality, as in *The House of All Nations* but sometimes of a
shocking originality, as in *Cotters' England*. The resistance
Stead's art has posed to accommodation within conventional
critical categories – whether high modernist, bourgeois
realist, socialist realist, or feminist – makes her an extremely
important subject for critics and theoreticians looking for

more satisfying ways of understanding how we read and how canons have been formed. She has been neither assimilated nor forgotten. She remains a challenge to us all.

3 Finding a Voice

Unlike most of her family who were hearty singers, Stead records that she herself had a weak speaking voice that forced her to turn from the classroom to the correspondence course in her work as a teacher. As a writer too, her voice is muted. Whereas many writers stamp their work with the unmistakeable quality of their own articulation, Stead's stamp is the flexibility with which she allows her characters to speak through her. She wrote not so much to impose her vision as to release the voices she heard clamouring to be spoken in the world around her. For her, writing was an act of attention first of all, of listening, then enabling other voices to speak through her and attempting to understand them.

Seven Poor Men of Sydney: Releasing new voices

Seven Poor Men of Sydney, Stead's first published novel, begins conventionally, locating its story in a carefully established place and time, which it identifies as well suited to 'an old tale'.[1] At first, this old tale seems to be the familiar story of a sensitive young boy's growing up and away from his parents' ideas. In this section, the tradition seems to be writing Stead, as if she had to work its influence out of her system, and out of her readers', before she could move on to what really interested her – the relations between individuals, not the individual in his or her own self. Like many women writers before her, she casts her own growing up in the masculine mode, investing her experience in the male character Michael Baguenault and assuming an omniscient but vaguely male-sounding voice for her narration.

This voice recounts Lawrentian passages of communion with nature under the aegis of the 'dead eye of the lunar world' (p. 13) and scenes reminiscent of George Eliot where Michael preaches to his schoolmaster: 'How blunt our senses are, how many thick veils hang between us and the world. How will we ever refine our eyes to see atoms and our ears to hear the messages of ants?' (p. 17). Here the rebellion against the generating English tradition begins. Michael's conclusions contradict George Eliot's. Where she saw order as the determining principle of the natural world, he sees disorder, a disorder the novel increasingly comes to mirror as it starts defying the narrative expectations it initially set up. Michael loses his centrality, disappearing for long stretches at a time, undergoing service in the First World War, various affairs, and a nervous breakdown offstage. The reader learns of these events long after they have occurred, through hearsay.

As it proceeds, the novel launches itself defiantly against the 'comic-opera conventions' of official art, denounced by Baruch Mendelssohn (p. 242) to his appreciative audience, the dissatisfied 'ne'er-do-weel' Michael. Instead of heroes and villains performing individual feats, *Seven Poor Men* follows a community of characters whose interactions are its subject. Elaborately structured about a circle of friends and relatives, *Seven Poor Men* explores the links maintained by blood and friendship, shuttling back and forth between the Baguenaults' home in the suburbs and their cousin Joseph's workplace, the almost bankrupt print shop in town. Stead shows how these two settings, normally opposed, also resemble one another in that both are sites of production. The family produces and socialises workers to maintain the status quo, while the print shop reinforces and continues this process.

But in *Seven Poor Men*, Michael and his older sister

Catherine resist their parents' pleas to marry, settle down, and reproduce their parents' pattern of living. Significantly, this rejection involves denying the father; in *Seven Poor Men* becoming a literal denial of his paternity when Michael learns to his joy that he is a bastard. In a phrase reminiscent of ancient fertility cult ritual, Michael gloats: 'Then the old orchid-king is not my papa' (p. 21). Having several times wished his father dead, Michael now discovers his wish come true. In this passage, Stead frees herself vicariously from the weight of paternal authority and her irksome dependence on it. This symbolic death of the father, accomplished through the mother's betrayal, sets the children free to become their own parents, to create their own selves in the world. And imaginatively it sets Stead free to shape her own fictions as she pleases.

Just as Michael and Catherine's rebellion denies authority to the father in the home, so the workers' dissatisfaction with the inequality of their lot and their boss's own incompetence deny paternal authority in the workplace. Even the simple Joseph Baguenault, Michael and Catherine's cousin, and the chief representative of what a Marxist would call 'false consciousness' in the novel, when asked who works harder, his boss or himself, is forced to admit that he and his fellow workers work harder, and so begins to question the fairness of the division of money the business brings in. When Baruch asks rhetorically, 'How does a small minority oppress a large majority?' (p. 193), he is stating the novel's chief concern. Stead sees women as oppressed by the same paternalistic system, supported by the Church, that oppresses the novel's poor working people. Most of the novel devotes itself to answering Baruch's question, locating the answer in short-term perceptions of financial need and unquestioning acceptance of ruling orthodoxies that deny initiative to the oppressed.

Although Joseph Baguenault provides the tenuous link connecting these two sites – the home and the workplace –

he is far from forming the novel's centre of attention, which deliberately shifts our gaze from the individual personality to the interlocking lines of connection between people: between parent and child, boss and worker, brother and sister, boyfriend and girlfriend, teacher and student, priest and parishioner, husband and wife. These and various forms of friendship – tutelary, exploitative, worshipful, disinterested – create the dynamics of *Seven Poor Men*. What Michael continually tries and fails to see – that moment of change when one thing becomes another, the transformations that create life – Stead recreates in her narrative so that her readers may see. Michael suspects that life is not 'a succession of dead, shed moments without inter-relation' (p. 17); it is a continuous flux of transformations linking everything. Baruch puts it best when he tells Joseph: 'Conversation is the fire of social life, and see how it dies; nothing remains but a few bitter ends to sear some poor souls' (p. 141). Stead sets herself this paradoxical task of reviving these dying flames of oral art in her writing. 'The fire of social life' is her true subject – and how it burns through words. No wonder she has developed unconventional structures to convey such a theme. A conventional focus on a single individual would distort her knowledge that the isolated individual is an illusion. Context is all.

Seven Poor Men also burns with the irony that all the old oppressive ways of thinking and the institutions that continue them should have been transported to Australia from abroad. Instead of adopting the mythology of freedom that capitalism projects, and that the novel demonstrates is purely illusory, Australians might have started afresh and created a truly free society of equals. If only they could have shed the father, that symbol of patriarchal authority, as easily as Michael sheds his. What went wrong? This recurrent theme reaches full expression in Kol Blount's 'In Memorium' on Michael's death (pp. 305–9). The

Australian social context, with its memory of transported rebels shipped out from the Old World to punishment in the New, promotes a questioning that none of the novel's authority figures can quell.

Similarly, because the 1920s in Sydney as elsewhere were a time of social ferment and questioning, the events of *Seven Poor Men* are the public occasions when people meet to thrash out their positions with regard to these new ideas: night school, public lectures, political meetings, picnics and parties. This series of elaborately connected events, formed by disintegrating and growing patterns of relationship, replace the focus on order, often represented by the maturing of a single individual, that distinguishes the novels canonised in F. R. Leavis' Great Tradition of English fiction. Stead's innovations may prove disconcerting to a reader accustomed to linear narrative or at least to a plot where the significance of each detail is never in doubt.

Stead gives her readers the sense she is plunging them into what Michael Baguenault terms 'the unwoven raw material of life' (p. 211). Yet this is only another illusion, produced through manipulation of the web of words all verbal conjurers use. Stead seeks to show us the interweaving of the threads themselves rather than the design they form, the texture of the weave rather than the completed web, to draw attention to processes of production rather than to the artifact that has been produced. This metaphor of the 'close and tangled web' of an ordinary family's inner life (p. 2) begins and ends her story, assuming larger dimensions as the illusory web of Maya in the endpiece, where 'the threads of the mesh appear and are woven of the bodies of flying men and women with the gestures interlocked in thousands of attitudes of passion . . . Now the web trembles, now the threads are free and they swing out into space . . .' (pp. 317–18). Stead employs this cliché of the web of life to help us see it with fresh

eyes, as something made and therefore not inevitable, as
something that both reveals truths and hides them,
providing an illusory structure for an inherent disorder – as
does a novel. As do, in fact, all the social structures we
tend to take for granted, including capitalist paternalism's
misogyny.

Seven Poor Men dramatises a world in ferment, where all
the old truths are being questioned: Christianity, pre-
Darwinian science, capitalism, even sexism. Yet of all this
repressive old system the new age is rejecting, sexism
appears the most firmly entrenched kind of blindness.
Indeed, for a reader sensitised to notice such things, the
vicious misogyny of this world is striking. And far from
providing an alternative to traditional Christianity's violence
against women, the new bohemianism seems merely to
extend it in new directions. Every work of art the young
characters encounter presents an image of woman as an
object to be appreciated or violated. 'Liberation' in radical
circles means posing nude for 'artists', making love
indiscriminately and expecting nothing in exchange, making
tea and posters for political gatherings at which men will
speak. 'Woman' is a term of abuse: the priest courting
Michael's weak mother for the church is dismissed as a
'woman' (p. 18); Withers' degeneracy seems proved by his
'womanly' nature (pp. 25, 26, 92). Women themselves are
described as mothers, old maids, odalisques, whores or
'nice little bits of fluff' (p. 45). We are continually reminded
of women's financial dependency, of their vulnerability to
sexual assault or abandonment, and of how few options
there are for a woman of talent who wants to earn her own
way. Whenever a woman tells her own story, it is always
one of frustration and defeat: Michael's mother, Joseph's
mother, Kol's mother, the old woman in the park whose
story so impresses Withers. Only Michael's sister Catherine
still fights what she refuses to believe is her fate, although
it is hardly promising that we should last see her voluntarily

committed to a lunatic asylum, plunging a knife into her
wrist to impress Baruch with her courage.

Withers, probably the novel's least likable character,
expresses his society's fear of and hatred for women in his
reaction to Catherine: 'She's like one of those female
spiders that eat their husbands. You're her brother, but
they don't recognise family relations, those man-eating
ladies' (p. 38). After a conversation with Mrs Baguenault,
he tells Michael: 'Come along out o' this. This collection of
skirts will drive you dippy before they've finished; one
with her religion, the other with her reds. What a woman's
man you are! Why don't you get a real woman and taste
their real goods, not all this eyewash?' (p. 38). The crude
reductiveness of Wither's thinking and the violence in his
language that so clearly expresses a deeply-rooted fear
condemn him more surely than any authorial commentary
could. By refusing to comment, Stead reminds us how
representative of current attitudes, even today, and how
unquestioned, until very recently, such speech has been.
The characters of *Seven Poor Men* live in a world where
such thinking is taken for granted. They find it natural for
whores to accost them in the street, for women to commit
suicide if they get pregnant out of wedlock, for women to
walk in fear of rape, to see everywhere in 'art' images of
their naked, often distorted, bodies.

Almost every character in the book is allowed his or her
speech on what was still then termed 'the woman problem'.
The cumulative effect of regurgitated cliché reveals a
complacent society, incapable or uninterested in seeking
truth. This collective voice pronounces judgement without
needing to think, even on those actions designed to disturb
its complacency, such as suicide. When yet another man
goes over the Gap, this voice easily assimilates his action
into its collective scheme of how things should be: 'A
suicide at the Gap was a commonplace affair. Everyone
knew why a person committed suicide: if it was a man,

because he couldn't pay his bills or had no job; if a woman, because she was going to have a baby' (p. 70). The action in *Seven Poor Men* flatly contradicts such folk wisdom. It denies that suicide is ever 'a commonplace affair'. When Michael goes over the Gap near the novel's end, Stead's readers have learned that suicide is a mysterious, complex and troubled affair, an action both individual and social in its origins and impact, something that cannot be explained by simple recourse to the 'logic' of economics or biology.

Seven Poor Men's feminism emerges in a similarly indirect fashion. The stupidity, sentimentality or limited experience of the speaker tends to qualify the pronouncement on 'woman's place' at the outset, predisposing the reader to reject what is said without feeling manipulated or preached at by a feminist author. Baruch is the only character not undermined by authorial presentation in this way. Instead, his intelligence and perception are continually borne out by action in the text as well as recognised by numerous characters within it. Whenever Baruch speaks, his pronouncements carry weight, whether or not they receive authorial commentary at the time. Baruch's contribution to the debate on the 'eternal man–woman question' at Kol's party corresponds most clearly to the state of affairs revealed in the novel as a whole. Baruch asserts that sexual differences are merely used as a blind to conceal a socioeconomic problem.' "There are no women," he interjects. "There are only dependent and exploited classes, of which women make one. The peculiarities are imposed on them to keep them in order. They are told from the cradle to the grave, You are a female and not altogether there, socially and politically: your brain is good but not too good, none of your race was ever a star, except in the theatre. And they believe it. We all believe these great social dogmas" ' (p. 205). Here Baruch anticipates Simone de Beauvoir's argument in *The Second Sex*, that women are 'made' not 'born'.

However, it is one thing to recognise the fact of this making, and quite another to undo it. Catherine successively goes through each of the positions possible for a woman who rejects the conditions of her society's 'making'. She denies the 'female charm' that her first boyfriend Milt Dean praises, by making herself into a monster, going about with holes in her stockings, unwashed hair and unbecoming clothes, only to discover that she has rejected being cast as 'angel in the house' merely in order to be cast instead as 'witch', 'old hag' or 'gypsy'. These too are theatrical roles, acceptable for the rebellious woman and therefore unacceptable for anyone trying to define an individual sense of self. The gypsy is as easily assimilated into patterns of exploitation as is the angel in the house. Witness the drawing of Catherine as an 'emaciated naked woman lying dead on the guays, while a curious crowd with caricature faces hung over it' (p. 36). Again this woman lying dead on the quays, while a curious crowd for' (p. 59), finds herself turned into an object, made an 'it', in the imagination of those she thought were her friends. She turns to socialist politics, recognising that her sex makes her an exploited class, only to discover the capitalist oppression of women duplicated in socialist circles.

Baruch's drawing, inspired by Catherine's visit to him, stresses her internalisation of society's definitions. In his depiction, although naked and wounded, she is still alive and fighting. When Joseph asks, 'What does it mean?', Baruch answers: 'Woman escapes from the forest. It means, the middle-class woman trying to free herself, and still impeded by romantic notions and ferocious, because ambushed, sensuality' (p. 155). A little later, Catherine comes to a similar recognition: 'I've fought all my life for male objectives in men's terms. I am neither man nor woman, rich nor poor, elegant nor worker, philistine nor artist. That's why I fight so hard and suffer so much and get nowhere' (p. 214). Her sense of self contradicts all the available definitions; there are no terms in which she can express what she is or what she wants. A choice between dualities, each of which depends for its very existence on its opposite, on that which it is not, is not really a choice at all. She does not want to be a woman, as traditionally defined, yet she does not want to be a man either. Yet society can only see her as one or the other. Significantly, her very strength makes Joseph see her as somehow masculine (pp. 254 and 265). Rationality has painted her into a corner, from which irrationality alone seems to offer her an escape. Madness transcends duality, seeking connections where logic denies them. As her brother Michael puts it early in the novel: 'the maniac was merely too much awake' (p. 10).

Catherine, Michael, Baruch and Kol are each in his or her own ways 'too much awake' for a somnolent society that depends for its hegemony on keeping people asleep. They each see beyond the commonly accepted proprieties, mouthed so threateningly or so pitifully by the novel's series of defeated, monster mothers and by Joseph before Baruch, with Winters' help, awakens him. Stead writes her fear of failure into each of their fates. Catherine's 'madness', Michael's suicide, Kol's paralysis and Baruch's flight to America embody her uncertainty at this stage of her career about whether she will be strong enough to rewrite the tradition in her own voice.

The images used to characterise Michael's restlessness with the world he is inheriting recur throughout Stead's work, later ascribed to female characters, always reflecting her own most intense preoccupations, preoccupations we can identify in part as springing from her situation as a woman writer challenging a masculine system of designating meaning. The hall of mirrors and the sons of Clovis, recurrent images first introduced here, are two versions of the dead end. All Stead's work can be seen as an attempt to escape that fate.

The hall of mirrors invokes the curse of solipsism. To be trapped in the self, unable to reach outward to another human being, unable even to be sure of their separate existence from your observing consciousness, is the hellish state suffered by all Stead's famous egotists. Michael describes it here as being 'like a man walking through a hall of mirrors and seeing a thousand reflections of himself on every side, each one a shell of himself, and insubstantial' (p. 17). The second image presents a different trap, that of paralysis and the subsequent inability to act or to create. The picture of 'The Sons of Clovis', hamstrung and drifting down a river toward their deaths, strikes Michael and his paralysed friend Kol Blount as an emblem of themselves. When we know that the sons of Clovis, whose picture hangs in the Sydney Art Gallery where it forcibly impressed Stead as a girl, were hamstrung by their father yet continue to remain loyal to him, then we can understand Michael's dream linking visions of his father 'lying in a pool of blood' with the painting (p. 207). And we can understand as well, the source of this painting's hold over Stead's imagination. Failure to separate oneself from the father, and the traditional authority he represents, will lead to paralysis and death. The break must be made.

Kol's fate seems to corroborate this reading. Paralysed from birth but tended by a loving mother, who invests all her emotional energies in him, Kol seems on the point of being cured at the novel's end. What had appeared admirable devotion on the mother's part is now described as 'a pure case of neglect and poverty' (p. 310). Just as Mrs Blount's nut and pickle sandwiches, meant to nourish, in fact make Michael sick, so all the care offered her son only serves to keep him paralysed. Familial ties of emotion more often serve to dominate than to succour. Trapped herself in an uncongenial role, the mother seeks to repeat her entrapment in her children. The pool of blood, representing the horror and the fascination of patricide, seems the only way to break this chain.

These images of defeat are balanced by visions of escape: Baruch's etching of Catherine fleeing the forest; his own flight to America; the news that Kol may possibly be cured; the final image of Joseph, having left his parents' home at last to form his own, finding his voice to tell his own story in his own way. Joseph, that 'letter of ordinary script' (p. 316) who throughout the novel marvelled at the easy command of language wielded by others, always sitting in silence himself, confused and humiliated, with nothing but his store of meaningless Latin tags memorised from school, is released into speech on a moonlit night with his wife as audience. The story he proceeds to tell will not be the *Seven Poor Men* we have just read but rather another version of the same events, filtered through a different angle of vision. In storytelling as in memory, nothing lives the same way twice. But Joseph has found a voice to speak what he knows, just as in writing *Seven Poor Men* Stead herself had begun to find a voice for describing life as she saw it.

From the outset, *Seven Poor Men* has seethed with an undercurrent of gagged voices seeking expression. Michael, 'inarticulate in his love affairs', hears 'long conversations carried on between his teeth and his tongue, between the towel and the washstand, the mosquito and the ceiling he was hitting' (p. 14), just as Stead reports she did as a child.[2] Later, his appropriately named friend, Chaunter, makes the entire natural world sing a fantastic composition for him (pp. 269–70), releasing those suppressed voices into symphonic expression. In the fantastic composition of *Seven Poor Men*, Stead frees the voices haunting her, making her 'old tale' new and her own.

The Salzburg Tales: **Ventriloquist's tricks**

Stead's first novel circumvented inherited English traditions of writing by locating its 'old tale' in a New World setting that was profoundly hostile to traditional authority. The new voices of an ancient continent unleashed in *Seven Poor Men* created their own subversive structure that undermined the traditional European privileging of order above flux, boss above worker and male above female. Her second book (although it was published a few months earlier) takes an entirely different tack. *The Salzburg Tales* swallows European traditions whole, showing she can write that way if she pleases. Her innovations elsewhere are deliberate; but here she is content to imitate – to demonstrate her often dazzling skill as a ventriloquist, allowing the tradition's old voices to speak through her.

The Salzburg Tales are chiefly interesting for what they show of a young writer testing her talent and searching for her style. Stead is not primarily a teller of short tales: her imagination needs space to work to advantage, for her interest is in context and in changing patterns of relation over time. Although *The Salzburg Tales* brings together a group of people to show their interactions in response to the challenge of the storytelling act itself, this potential for an extended exploration of storytelling traditions, both oral and written, remains embryonic only.

Several of Stead's recurring preoccupations emerge in these stories. Here she recreates the power of destructive loves, for other people or for money; the character who betrays early ideals for enjoyment of the 'amenities'; and the figure of the prodigal father, in 'Marionettist' and 'Overcote'. 'The Gold Bride' provides an economical linking of the fetishisation of gold and the objectification of women. But without the contexts provided by other lives and multiple perspectives, these preoccupations lose their power to compel. The schoolboy's impatient response to

the Old Man's patronising misogyny, masquerading as
such attitudes often do, behind a sentimentalising of
'women's charm', seems to promise a shift in perspective to
a questioning of old clichés. ' "Men, women", the schoolboy
cries, "they are the same animal: do we have to use these
old gaslight distinctions of man, woman, day and night
empiry, these suspect gallantries overscented to conceal
bad odours! There are only two kinds in our society, rich,
poor, master, servant, proprietor and pensioner; and all
the foibles of women that we laugh at in secret, are the
foibles of a dependent class." '[3] While his ideas also
oversimplify, they are preferable to the misogyny of the
others. But the men overrule him and the Old Man's
mawkish ramblings proceed.

Although most are interesting stories, they lack the
multi-dimensional qualities of Stead's great work. They
seem mere raw material awaiting development, deprived of
a context that could make them meaningful. Here Stead's
fascination for the flow of speech overcomes organising
principles of value. Most typical is the Musical Critic's
Tale, an overheard monologue at the Opera offered up as a
'found' story, perhaps not coincidentally a 'story' composed
of a mother's lament on how time and her children have
passed her by. Her attempt to use her helplessness to
manipulate her son and his lover is echoed by many other
women in Stead's later fiction but there it is 'placed' in
relation to the choices made by other characters. Here it is
simply recorded. The teller's passion for eavesdropping,
that makes of him a 'connoisseur of what people say in the
dark' (p. 368), is clearly also Stead's. But the connoisseur
must be more than just a tape recorder. At her best, Stead
lets us hear not only how people sound but also what their
voices tell us about their lives. In her later work, Stead
seldom crosses the fine line separating the authentic from
the tedious. Here her balance wavers.

Even more problematic are the stories, also included

without commentary, that take for their subject matter society's outright violence toward women. The moral of the Musician's Tale, disguised as love, expresses a threat: 'What is wilder, more reckless and weaker than a rebellious woman? History, reason and intuition all tell her she must fail in this world of men' (p. 333). This is the erroneous conclusion he draws from a tale of the rape, robbery and murder of an ardently serious young female musician. He blames the victim. And no one offers an alternative interpretation. Similarly, the teller and audience of 'The Triskelion', a blood-curdling tale of sexual abuse within the family, utterly miss the point of the story – the corrupt ways in which the law and the business world conspire together to protect the oppressor from the consequences of his crimes. Again they tend to blame the victim and express titillation rather than horror at the story's revelations of corruption.

Stead's refusal to comment in these instances (or to place them through the reactions of other characters) must be taken as at least a kind of endorsement, which suggests either her own participation in the blindness of her characters at this point or her uncertainty about how to express moral judgement without appearing propagandistic. Probably the answer lies in some combination of the two. Women have long been trained not to identify with their sex. Inherited discourse, as these stories prove, discourages such an identification, disqualifying its insights from the ranks of acceptable criticism. Indeed, these stories present the vast store of our legacy from the past – folktales, saints' lives, realistic narrative, tales of magic and of business – as all one-dimensional, whether told by a man or a woman, because they all lack a woman's point of view.

In writing *Seven Poor Men of Sydney* Stead found it natural to write of Australia in an Australian voice, distrustful of European authority and eager to create a literature more suited to Australian realities. But in *The*

Salzburg Tales she seeks to locate herself within the European traditions appropriate to her new environment. The result is accomplished but conventional. She has a good ear, can tell a good story but here suppresses the original critical intelligence that springs from her own experience as a woman and that gives her work its disturbing power elsewhere. Yet *The Salzburg Tales* do reveal the corrupt complacency of an establishment that marginalises women, the poor and the colonised. As a member of each of these three groups, Stead brought with her an experience that did not find itself reflected in the European literary traditions that animate *The Salzburg Tales*, so that they could only represent a dead end in her search for her own literary style.

4 Parisian Affairs

At first glance Stead's two Parisian novels, published in the late thirties, appear to have nothing whatever in common except for the city of their location. *The Beauties and Furies* could be her *Madame Bovary*; *House of All Nations* her *Comédie Humaine*. The first focuses on private lives and sexual affairs; the second on public lives and business affairs. Yet each novel questions these arbitrary divisions, showing the ways in which public and private interact and reflect one another.

The Beauties and Furies: Becalmed off Cythera

The interlockings of a series of triangular relationships provide a skeletal structure underpinning the linguistic explorations of *The Beauties and Furies*. The central triangle is formed by Elvira Western's adulterous affair with Oliver Fenton, a young student she joins in Paris, leaving her older husband Paul behind in England. The novel begins with her journeying toward Oliver in Paris and ends after she has abandoned him to rejoin her husband, with Oliver travelling back to England to look for a job. These two symmetrical train journeys, marking moments of decision, frame the long periods of indecision and mental wanderings to and fro between different positions that form the substance of the novel. These indecisions themselves take shape as choices between people and the options they seem to represent, yet in a very real sense the novel is about indecision in a world where there are no real choices. In

Marpurgo's words, these characters remain 'becalmed off Cytherea'.[1]

Stead wrote the novel at a time when she had already made her own decisions. She had left an earlier young man who had treated her badly to accompany her boss, William Blake, to Paris, where they were working out together what kind of a relationship they would have. In *The Beauties and Furies*, Stead explores the options she chose not to follow in her life. In many ways this novel seems the negative of the later autobiographical *For Love Alone*, which was, however, also begun at this time. Both Teresa and Elvira follow a selfish young student overseas, find their hopes for fulfilment through him disappointed and turn to an older man instead. But the differences are more interesting than the similarities. Because Elvira is more conventional than Teresa, defining herself according to how she imagines others see her, her story unlike Teresa's, is largely told from the outside, through its reflections in a series of other triangular relationships.

Elvira is torn between the fatherly Paul and the juvenile Oliver, who seems her twin, a reflection of herself but also of her wayward brother Adam. Paul himself is torn between Elvira, in every way his opposite, and his cousin Sara, who resembles him. Coromandel forms a triangle with her father and her mother, who is jealous of the close bond between father and daughter. All these relationships are incestuous. Oliver wanders from one woman to another. And with a finger in the pie of all these relationships there remains the mysterious Annabale Marpurgo. He himself is torn between his frail, childlike wife Clara and the robust Coromandel; and between Antoine and Georges Fuseaux. Like Elvira, he is frustrated by his failure to create, while despising those who have 'fooled' themselves into careers. Oliver sees him as Disorder incarnate, yet he functions much as the artist herself does, manipulating and dissecting relationships for his own and our amusement.

Each of these characters embodies a universe of self-absorption which, seeking to absorb the other into its own orbit, calls the process 'love'. Yet while Elvira grows cynical about the self-interest inherent in love, Stead herself delights in the comedy and variety of its manifestations. Like Coromandel, this novel gets carried away by the sheer sound of words and the display of fantasy. Like Elvira discovering her sensuality, Stead's writing strikes dramatic poses and caresses her words – in general, conducts a love affair with the language. For the reader, much of what results is ridiculous. Marpurgo's tortured prose, Oliver's parodies, many of the abrupt excursions into fantasy – these fail miserably; and fortunately, this is the last novel in which such experiments occur for Stead discovers here the dialectical style most appropriate to her vision.

Paris provides the context. In Marpurgo's words, 'She has many beauties – and furies' (p. 226). The romantic interplay of opposites suggested here sets the novel's tone and theme. It explores the mythology of the tourist's Paris – Anglophones gossiping in cafés, students working in the Archives, a night life of restaurants, hotels, cabarets and prostitutes. Through the Fuseaux brothers' business, we glimpse another world of work, but their Paris is reserved for Stead's next novel, *The House of All Nations*. Yet the elements destined to become compelling in one of Stead's masterpieces fail to ignite in this apprenticeship work. Here their dramas remain subordinate to Stead's interest in male/female relationships. As Marpurgo remarks self-consciously near the end of the novel, 'There is always someone who suffers in this kind of story. In every grouping, there is the untold tale' (p. 369). Although he is thinking of Sara, his remarks also apply to the Fuseaux business and to Stead's work generally. She can never forget 'the untold tale' lying silent beneath that told. Sometimes these untold tales erupt into the text through dreams or apparent digressions; yet for the writer who believes that nothing can exist independent of its contexts, it follows that nothing can really be a digression. Everything connects.

The transformations the lace business is undergoing from fine craftsmanship to mass-produced work of inferior quality, reducing the workers from craftsmen and women to replaceable cogs in an impersonal system, create repercussions in other areas of human life. Elvira thinks of her lovers in much the same way the industrialist Boutdelaize thinks of his workers. She chooses Oliver as her lover 'just as an experiment' (p. 79), because she believes 'all men are the same, practically' (p. 80). This cold-blooded confession freezes Oliver's spontaneity, but the attitude it betrays is also responsible for much of Elvira's own malaise. If she cannot believe in the unique existence of others, neither can she believe in her own.

The letter from Oliver which spurs her flight to Paris describes her as a Sleeping Beauty, begging 'Oh, do wake up, come to life before it is too late: before the thorns interlock and crib you forever' (p. 3). Like the princess in the tale, she seems to need a rescuing prince to awaken her from her long suburban sleep and an audience before she can act. Although she writes to her husband, bragging 'I am taking my freedom' (p. 6), we learn to see her as enslaved to social convention, eager for approval, at once insecure and opinionated in her insecurity. She does not know how to take her freedom because she cannot imagine such a state.

An early exchange with Oliver comments indirectly on Elvira's situation. When he wonders why the French working people go on with their burdens, when 'They only have to lay them down and they are free. Why do they go on?', Elvira answers irritably: 'Why? Because they're hungry and tired and their wives won't let them leave their jobs' (p. 11). Through Elvira's story, the novelist asks herself a similar question – why do women acquiesce in their subjection to men? – and provides a similar answer – because they believe, however wrongly, that it is in their material interests to do so. As Elvira remarks nastily near the end of her affair with Oliver: 'That's why the marriage system holds up under all the attacks. The profits are better than free love' (p. 345). For a woman who finds her linen more satisfying than her lovers, this maxim holds true. Her love of property prompts Elvira to choose dependency over freedom. Again she tells Oliver: 'I can live parasitically and I will' (p. 276). In making this choice she joins all Stead's sellouts, those characters whom Adam Constant in *The House of All Nations* terms, 'side-tracked talents', the people who betray their ideals for some share in the 'amenities'. Oliver is her counterpart in this trait as well, explaining to Marpurgo that he has chosen a safe thesis topic because he wants 'to look like a socialist who knows the amenities' (p. 26).

But in choosing property over humanity, they acquiesce in the reduction of their own status to that of property. Elvira 'sells' herself on the marriage market; Oliver 'sells' himself on the 'free' business market. Incident after incident draws attention to the frank money philosophy of the French, best expressed in Paris, which Oliver celebrates as 'the land of enchantment . . . where there are more false diamonds and false eyelashes than anywhere else, where the gowns are more elegant, the complexions more enamelled, laces finer, shoes smaller, heels higher, the gait more billowy, the fans better painted and the breasts set more to advantage than in all the world' (p. 18). In other words, Paris is the ultimate woman as object, the painted whore, in whose image he hopes to remake Elvira (p. 13). She first appears 'slipping her new shoe off her swollen right foot' (p. 1). This 'shoe' is too confining a fit. Oliver tells Coromandel that 'Every woman is the headless woman: we love the Venus without an arm, the leaf-winged hamadryad . . .' (p. 186), again the woman as object. Yet on another occasion he is capable of lamenting to Elvira: 'I love to think of a state in which women will be perfectly free. The women we know are inchoate . . . Aphrodite is not yet born' (p. 85). *The Beauties and Furies* suggests that this birth will not come to pass until men and women alter their economic relations, ceasing to see prostitution as romantic and the objectification of women in shows like the Folies Bergères as satisfying, 'like a good French dinner' (p. 109).

Not only does Elvira see herself as an object, a 'cabbage-wife' or a sensuous body, but she also sees other women in the same degrading terms because she has been educated to see herself and others through male eyes. This novel suggests, however, that it is not just through male eyes but more specifically through advanced capitalist eyes. The numerous discussions of reducing the world to a 'pauper economy' held at the Fuseaux' and in *The House of All Nations* at the Bertillons', are not digressions; they illustrate the philosophy that pervades all human relations in our present economic system. Men and women prey on one another and call it 'love' in private relationships because men and women prey on one another and call it 'business' in public relations. Just as the quality of the lace deteriorates as the profits increase, so the quality of the love deteriorates when the lovers' attention is diverted from the act itself to what they can get out of it for themselves. Oliver's, and Elvira's, real indifference to the interchangeability of their sexual partners corresponds to the interchangeability of workers in the mass production system. The uniqueness of everything in the Paindebled's antique shop represents values that can never be assimilated into such a world. The lace umbrella cover is one of the few priceless creations left in a world where most people believe that not only everything but also every person has its price. Similarly, the designs Coromandel's mother creates are beautiful, but

unsaleable; they are literally labours of love. And it is only
in making love with Coromandel in this special world, that
Oliver is able to make the earth itself shake in a magical
moment worthy of Angela Carter. The boundaries between
real and unreal are drawn differently in the Paindebled's
home because they themselves see the world differently
from the majority of the novel's characters.

The Beauties and Furies documents the contradictions
involved in choosing parasitism, and thus agreeing to one's
social definition as a commodity, in exchange for the
amenities. Angry at her helplessness, Elvira also cherishes
it and even cultivates it because it is her chief weapon for
manipulating her men. She blames them for her continuing
unhappiness with the choice she has made. And she is
right, of course, about the many extra obstacles blocking a
woman's path to independence. With an Honours M.A.
she is just as well-educated as Oliver yet he continually
insults her intelligence, remarking for example on their
first night together that he 'is surprised' that Elvira 'had
the brains' to pick up the entertaining Marpurgo (p. 17)
and later making such affectionate remarks as 'You're such
an idiot, I have to love you' and, when she tells him to stop
playing 'her Messiah', answering 'All right, I promise to let
you go on being your own little dud self – for a while'
(p. 93). Because such male condescension determines the
way the world is run, her economic opportunities are much
more limited than his. Although she has a university
degree, Sara's efficiency is confined to running a lunchroom
while Adam is free to ruin several much better managerial
positions. Similarly, Oliver looks forward to a professorial
position, while the best Elvira could do with her school
prizes and M.A. is work as a secretary.

Her pregnancy leads her to complain: 'It's degrading to
be a woman, to have to bother about what people think,
not to be able to provide for your child, to be dependent
on men' (p. 130). And later, summing up her thinking,

'The real thought of the middle-class woman . . . is the problem of economic freedom and sexual freedom: they can't be attained at the same time' (p. 131). While all these complaints are just, we can also see that Elvira herself is too lazy and too imbued with the derogatory conventional mythology of 'woman's nature', to fight very hard against what she sees as her 'fate'. Her conversation with Coromandel reveals her complacency. ' "If I had a function I could organise my life better," claims Elvira. "You could easily get one," laughs Coromandel' (p. 314). ' "I have had two husbands, and it is lonely", complains Elvira. "I am sorry," [says] Coromandel, "but I cannot feel lonely even alone" ' (p. 315). Clearly Elvira wants to feel sorry for herself. Her egotism has seized on mythologies of women's dependence and uses them to gain attention. Coromandel's confident independence puzzles Elvira while Elvira's 'suggestive, mournful, bovine, breeding look' burdens Coromandel (p. 317). Elvira is surprised that Coromandel would think of marrying. 'Do you want to give up your independence for a man?' she asks. 'I never thought of it that way' replies Coromandel (p. 315). They have been talking at cross purposes.

Coromandel provides positive alternatives to Elvira's despair that Elvira herself cannot imagine. Where Elvira blames everyone but herself for her troubles, Coromandel assumes full responsibility for all her actions. Oliver is surprised to find that she is not upset to discover that both he and Marpurgo had deceived her. She replies: 'I live and learn, that's all. I love living, I love learning: nothing will ever abate me' (p. 365). Coromandel, like Teresa in *For Love Alone*, refuses the dependent role to create her own independent sense of self and make her own destiny. In contrast, Elvira, like Miss Herbert, remains attached to her chains. She prefers men to women because she can manage them more easily, convincing them that they are responsible for her unhappiness.

Indeed, Paul irritates Elvira by his repeated insistence that she herself must make up her own mind; he will not decide for her. Oliver, on the other hand, delights in her helpless act, which flatters his self-importance as her disturbing honesty does not. Yet even Paul accepts responsibility where he should not, thinking 'I should have given her a profession; made her a doctor, or a laboratory assistant' (p. 151). As if independence were something one could give or make for another! Elvira's 'navel philosophy' is the technique devised by her 'prolific ego' (p. 177) to gain attention. She turns helplessness into a weapon to relieve her boredom. She never awakens from the sleep she has chosen. Stead presents her, not simply as an isolated individual, but as the representative of a class doubly trapped – the middle-class woman who accepts her chains in return for the amenities.

Critics have had trouble integrating the episode at the Somnambulists Club into the story of Elvira's adultery. The key lies in the imagery of sleeping and waking that is central in this novel as in much of Stead's work. The title suggests that sleeping beauties once awakened may turn into avenging furies, as Elvira herself does when she discovers that Oliver is another dead end for her hopes. But I have suggested that Elvira never really wakes, preferring, like Oliver, to remain in what Marpurgo calls a somnambulist state, sleepwalking through a life whose real horrors they choose not to see. Oliver dismisses the crackpot philosophy he hears as 'cuckoo lore' (p. 338), recalling Marpurgo's dismissal of talk on the train when he first meets Elvira as 'cuckoo-lore' (p. 4). Stead is punning on the popular association of the cuckoo with the cuckold but to serious as well as comic ends. Human beings betray not only one another but also themselves; most of us mistake our real interests, sleepwalking through the world confusing dreams with reality. As Elvira says, we tend to read into others what we want to see (p. 85). And Paul laments: 'We see so little in life, I don't like a sweeping opinion. We go through life erratically like a drunk motor-car turning its headlights this way and that, getting snatches of foliage. The true portrait of a person should be built up as a painter builds it, with hints from everyone, brush-strokes, thousands of little touches' (p. 159). The Somnambulists Club puts this theory into practice, refiltering events through a surrealist lens. Oliver has been reading Elvira James Joyce's *Ulysses*; as he gets drunk he relives his own Nighttown scene. Throughout the novel he has treated women as objects; now objects themselves take on voices to berate him. The clock, spittoon, carpet and footnotes find voices to speak of their oppression but Oliver dismisses this revelation as a drunken nightmare when he "wakes'. In his customary somnambulist state, he can live comfortably with the contradictions between his professed beliefs and his actions.

So can Elvira. Returning from her dream of finding freedom in Paris to her suburban sleep with Paul, she says she feels 'like someone coming back from the dead' (p. 373). Neither she nor Oliver wake from the claustrophobic world of the narcissist. The scene after her bath when Oliver watches her kissing and stroking her body before the mirror defines the extent of her sensuality. Looking inward rather than outward, she finds herself incapable of feeling love (p. 77). No Aphrodite will find birth here. The characters in *The Beauties and Furies* remain locked in their 'hall of mirrors' (p. 230). 'Lying becalmed off Cytherea' (p. 21), they will never reach the desired shores of the island of fulfilling 'spiritual adventures'. Readers must wait until *For Love Alone* to embark on the stormy voyage to Cythera with the iconoclastic Teresa Hawkins. *The Beauties and Furies* shows us dead souls, characters trapped in unsatisfactory roles from which they cannot awaken.

House of All Nations: **The bank as whorehouse**

Stead's third novel brings her chief interests – power, money and sex – together in the most concrete form yet, that of the bank as an international whorehouse, selling human beings as commodities, subordinating everything to the urge to accumulate surplus wealth. The title refers to a famous Paris whorehouse, mentioned twice in the narrative itself. Stead makes it clear that this bank is not an aberration but the logical expression of the capitalist system. Through the activities centred on the Banque Mercure, Stead reveals the very heart of the so-called 'man's world' – international finance – as a shoddy con job. Its 'free market' her characters confess to be a new and more efficient form of slavery; its laws rigged to protect organised corruption; its platitudes designed to keep ordinary people off the scent of its decomposition.

In a powerful chapter entitled 'J'Accuse', Adam Constant, the poet/bank clerk, outlines a dream which corresponds to Stead's achievement in writing this novel:

My dream is, that one day I will get them all down, I will leave them on record. I want to show the waste, the insane freaks of these money men, the cynicism and egotism of their life, the way they gambol amidst plates of gold loaded with fruits and crystal jars of liqueurs, meats pouring out juices, sauces, rare vegetables, fine fancy breads, and know very well what they are doing, brag, in fact, of being more cunning than the others, the poor. I'll show that they are not brilliant, not romantic, not delightful, not intelligent; that they have no other object but their personal success and safety. Although, of course, there are plenty of living intelligences among them, sidetracked talents, even warm breasts, perspicacious men amongst them, but all, all compliant and prostituted . . . .[2]

Here is Stead's novel in a nutshell. In detail after detail, she shows how the sensuous abundance of the earth is hogged and wasted by the few, who can only be summed up in a string of negatives for they have no positive existence. This drama of 'grab and graft' (p. 199) enacted as a 'gigantic, monstrous masque put on the boards to fool the people' (pp. 80–81), serves, when translated from life into art or masque into novel, to enlighten the people. The metaphor of prostitution, the selling of the self, defines our civilisation and explains how such a state of affairs can continue to exist. Stead excels in depicting the sellouts, the 'sidetracked talents', in showing why people allow themselves to be used and the many ways they fool themselves about the nature of their complicity, because she genuinely understands their dilemma. She sees ugliness but she also sees torment in even the most despicable lives. Her sympathy prevents *House of All Nations* from becoming a mere diatribe, while her intense sensitivity to the interconnections of context allows the novel to grow to enormous proportions. It is her longest book.

The accumulation of words piled up to reveal a hollow centre – the bankruptcy of purpose at the heart of twentieth-century capitalist society – mirrors the accumulation of stock-market accounts, designed to hide the emptiness of vaults, in the Banque Mercure, the House of All Nations. Scene builds on scene, character on character, image on image – all to reveal the emptiness underlying such apparent prodigality.

Stead herself was clearly fascinated by the superficial vitality of some of the participants, by their daredevil honesty in admitting their motivation and techniques, without the usual hypocrisy of the system, and by their underdog status as small capitalists, challenging hopeless odds in a time of the big international monopoly syndicates. They know they must crash eventually but would rather have a fling than plod along forever in a middle-class routine. Thus she presents Jules Bertillon as a modern-day Mercury, a high-flying god, someone more or less than human, a shadow, an illusion created by the play of light, and contrasts him favourably with the grossly overweight Raccamond, as substantial as Jules is insubstantial, and with the decadent Carrière, as depraved as Jules is wholesome.

Jules is an artist whose creativity has been turned by the system from building to the performing of magic tricks. Alphendéry calls him a 'spoiled artisan' (p. 197); he sees himself as a magician (p. 201). His enemies are the enemies of the human imagination everywhere: the sterility of the vicious and of the plodding. Jacques Carrière is Jules' nemesis because where Jules is 'endlessly primevally fertile', he is 'formless and cannot conceive properly' (p. 164). A depraved aristocrat and careerist politician (as his name, the French for career, implies), he is committed to destruction. His credo: 'To realize anything is vulgar' (p. 163). Ominously, rumours spread that a young boy was killed at one of his orgies. His lackey and pimp, the good bourgeois Raccamond, true to his name, brings ruin to Jules' world, through mistaking the illusion for reality. Because he lacks Jules' imagination and Carrière's intelligence, he fools himself with his hypocrisy, self-righteously destroying the bank he had hoped to grab for himself. Raccamond is the physical embodiment of all the 'Fat People', Haller's term for what Raccamond calls 'the sound bourgeoisie' (p. 289). Watching him stuff himself, gaining weight and suffering indigestion for his greed, the reader does not need Haller to tell her that 'there is something wrong when five per cent of the people stuff and ninety-five per cent have almost nothing to eat' (p. 289). In this novel, every form of vice finds convincing physical embodiment and contributes to the dénouement of the story – that of the bank's mercurial rise and inevitable fall.

If Carrière is Jules's demonic counterpart, Henri Léon

is an alter ego. Where Jules refuses to deal in anything substantial, preferring the illusory game of playing contre-partie with non-existent stock shares, Léon is a grain dealer who prefers to work with commodities. Substantial where Jules is transparent, earth where Jules is air, gregarious where Jules is a loner, Léon couples his creative genius with practical common sense, a trait that enables him to survive when Jules fails. Jules' betrayal of Léon's great wheat scheme is the saddest moment in the book because it shows a brilliant vision betrayed by petty stupidity. After this, we know that the bank's fall is inevitable but we will never again feel so deeply the futility of such flagrant waste.

In giving businessmen like Jules and Henri Léon such vibrant fictional life, Stead makes the perversions of their great talents her true tragedy. Her own creativity grieves to see its counterparts in the business world wasted in sterile games and turned to oppressive ends. At first glance, their recklessness seems endearing beside the calculated juggernaut advance of the multinationals and the despicable machinations of the petty blackmailer Raccamond. But the text as it proceeds reveals that very recklessness to be essential to the capitalist system, embodying as it does contempt for the individual human being and for the long-range survival of the human race.

Alphendéry alone seems to see the self-destruction inherent in this mad rush to accumulate at the expense of anything standing in one's path; yet seeing is not enough. Indeed, if Jules's 'side-tracked talent' gives the reader the 'tragedy' of the bank, whose rise and fall is determined by its owner's hubris, then Alphendéry's 'side-tracked talent' provides a parallel story, that of intellect, rather than creativity, led astray by its own form of pride. Alphendéry initially believes that he can work within the system without becoming corrupted; he learns too late that when one prostitutes one's talents, one becomes a prostitute and self-respect is no longer possible. The novel's final scene shows Alphendéry acting the part of Judas, denying his past beliefs in socialism, selling out for a poorly paid job as Léon's lackey. Contempt for others inevitably leads to contempt for the self.

A special contempt for women, as traditional scapegoat figures, seems built into this system at such a fundamental level that no one even notices it is there. Women still survive marginally as outdated modes of exchange between men in their bartering but the modern man clearly finds money much more interesting, reserving women for recreation in his off hours. As Jules points out, 'Raped money gets people much wilder than raped wives' (p. 351).

And if the social context proves stifling to men's creative instincts, it warps women's even more dramatically. The few standard roles always assigned her sex overwhelm any move toward claiming individuality. Several intelligent women play minor roles in the novel; each is reduced to a stereotypical function through the pressures and restrictions of circumstance. Marianne Raccamond, condemned to work through the inferior material of her husband's ambitions, destroys him and the bank through her attempts to intrigue as a modern Lady Macbeth. Adam Constant's jealous wife, Suzanne, similarly destroys everything she holds most dear. The ambitious American businesswoman, Margaret Weyman, 'succeeds' through prostituting herself as Henri Léon's mistress, just as Jules' wife, Claire-Josèphe, safeguards her financial position under the guise of playing the silly society matron. Even the great socialist leader Jean Frère's wife, Judith, cannot avoid being assigned a subsidiary role as anima. Her creative energies can inspire men and produce babies; the alternative is Suzanne's hysteria, Margaret's cynicism or Henrietta's silliness. The silent women, like Claire-Josèphe and Judith, earn Stead's approval along with the men's, but their effectiveness is severely limited when they are denied speech. On the other hand, in the novel's terms, the women who talk only do so to reveal their own ignorance of men's affairs or to express the pent-up violence of their frustrations, which nobody wants to hear. The context in which all these women find themselves allows them no further freedom than to choose by which of these rules, all loaded against them, they shall play the man's game. If they are smart and lucky, like Mrs Achitophelous and Margaret Weyman, they can occasionally beat the men at their own game but there is no question of changing the game. They can exchange masters but they can never be anything more than wife or 'mistress'.

The opening scene establishes this context, contrasting the seduction techniques of two businessmen, Henri Léon and Paul Méline, to link lying and seduction in sexual relations to the use of the same techniques in business. The moral values of this world are established at the outset: one does not distinguish between right or wrong, truth or falsehood; one distinguishes between success or failure. 'Whereas Léon had an old, dull story and began by telling girls that he was unhappy and misunderstood at home, Méline always showed a picture of his wife and raved about his domestic happiness. It put everyone on the right footing and kept him out of scrapes' (p. 6). The honest confession of self-interest proves a smarter con game than the obvious lie; the bank also operates on this system. Women are the dupes of the professional lovers' con games just as the customers of the bank are the sheep to be fleeced or the cows to be milked by the professional bankers. Indeed, women are 'cows' to Léon, who clearly believes it is much better to be a bull. As he points out, 'the worst thing you can say to a man is to call him a *femmelette*, puny woman' (p. 10). Officially Léon is in Paris to arrange the marriage of his daughter to a wealthy young bourgeois while unofficially he buys himself prostitutes at an astonishingly desperate rate.

Scene Three, 'Blind, Instinctive Love', reveals how

symmetrical these activities are, through the confrontation of Achitophelous and his rebellious daughter, for whom he is also thinking of arranging a marriage with the same eligible young man. She, however, rejects the arranged marriage, saying 'You are a white slaver. You want to buy and sell me' (p. 32). Metaphorically, this seems apt. Some 400 pages later, we learn that much of his money (and therefore his respectability) does indeed come from the white slave trade. The subjection of women literally provides the foundations of his fortune, as well as those of many other investors in the bank and by implication of the capitalist system it embodies.

Everything he says in reply to his daughter reveals how inescapably he sees her as an object in his possession which he has an inalienable right to dispose of as he sees fit, even as he protests his fatherly 'love'. 'Are you still a virgin? Can I give you to the son of my friend without being ashamed of myself?' And finally resorting to naked power: 'But I insist on it – blind, instinctive love. If you can't love me that way, you are no good to me. You can get out. You are no daughter. You are anybody's girl.' He cannot conceive of her as a person in her own right; either she belongs to him or 'anybody' – someone else. As he says to Jules, 'A son . . . is a gilt-edged security, but a daughter is goods that have to be given away with a bonus' (p. 37). These are not merely decorative figures of speech. The metaphors reveal how deeply all this society's values are steeped in commercial exchange, to the extent that what should be a means to an end, that is earning a living so that one may live, has taken over lives to become the sole end in itself. When a daughter is no longer a human being, but 'goods' to be manipulated, not only is her humanity denied in the process but also that of her father.

Yet Stead plays this scene, with its ugly implications, for comedy. Henrietta's speech and manners reveal her to be a silly young woman, parroting terms she does not really understand but knows will irritate her father. Stead reveals clearly that what these two characters think of as their individual personalities are really constructed for them by the social milieux in which they have come of age. Both are spoken by a ready-made language that does their thinking for them, making sure that Henrietta's adolescent rebellion will prove no more dangerous to the order of things than her father's old-fashioned expressions of paternalism. Alphendéry presents himself as the amoral manipulator of languages, bragging that he can convince either party of the rightness of the other's position. The visual dynamics of this scene, with the men winking at one another over Henrietta's head, reinforces their control over the entire situation – its physical context and its language – while underlining her helplessness. Yet at another level, they themselves are also pawns in the hands of larger interests. The novel depicts a world that has got out of hand, a system running the world merely in order to perpetuate itself, in which even revolutions serve establishment ends.

The following scene shows the wheat speculator Léon accumulating prostitutes in a bar, humiliating his middle-class women companions, merely to flaunt his power to do as he pleases, with people as counters. Léon collects women for the pleasure of increasing the numbers he can add to his score, not for sexual gratification which means little to him. Similarly Jules Bertillon piles up money, not for itself but to indicate how much further ahead he is than others in the game of life. Neither of these men are any longer capable of enjoying what their money can buy. Bored and restless, they know they are condemned to ever more frenzied activity: if they don't advance, they are falling behind.

Stead favours hectic subjects, characters and societies at points of crisis, in transition: she never shows a world at rest or a character in repose. Even stagnation is dynamic in her eyes, the senility of old Richard Plowman a continually

unfolding wonder of interest. And the 1930s provide the
perfect context for recording turmoil. The characters in
House of All Nations anxiously remember the Stock Market
Crash of 1929, the Russian Revolution, the First World
War, while fearfully discussing the rise of Hitler, the
Spanish and Chinese Revolutions, and the possible state of
the Gold Standard in England. When the bank finally fails,
Stead comments ironically that 'All the clients banded
themselves together in national protective associations, and
thus the next European war began in little' (p. 767). The
bank's story is Europe's story. Its rivalries, subterfuges,
plots and counterplots enact and illuminate the history of
Europe between the wars.

No one escapes unscathed from Stead's satirist's eye.
The self-righteous Englishman Stewart, superficially Jules'
opposite in every way, unconsciously reveals through his
own conversation the fundamental affinities underlying
their different techniques for the accumulation of capital.
Where Jules admits he is a wrecker, living off what he can
grab from a civilisation that is falling apart, seeing more
pickings for himself in times of unrest, Stewart believes
order makes for bigger profits. He argues that 'the worship
of the ruling classes saves money . . . . We do not have to
buy our servants. An Englishman is proud to serve'
(p. 334). He brags about how England absorbs and diverts
forces for change – a subject more fully explored in *Cotters'
England* – in exactly the same way that Jules brags that any
man can be bought at a price. Only the language and the
degree of self-awareness differ. As Jules comments when
Stewart leaves: 'The English are not hypocritical – it's not
true. They have a natural, ingrained double face from
birth!' (p. 336).

In this encyclopaedic anatomy of 'grab and graft', there
is only one small oasis of hope, where self-interest does not
seem to be the dominant principle – that is in Jean Frère
and his circle. Alphendéry and Constant are rejuvenated

by their contact with the Frères. They provide the only scenes in which characters escape the city for the country, in which simple wholesome food is served to satisfy real appetites, where people actually listen to what others are saying and where culture is something lived rather than bought. Frère's name, of course, reflects his beliefs in the brotherhood of man; he is a great socialist leader who seeks to better the lot of working people. His wife works with him and shares his beliefs. Yet although women's oppression is recognised along with that of other groups – workers, the colonised, blacks, children – in practice, her oppression seems ingrained even here. The wholesome stew that Jean and Judith prepared for their supper has been served out by Jean to all his male friends, so that there is nothing left for Judith or Suzanne when they arrive. This scene suggests their place in the socialist movement in France: they will always come last and the generosity will run out when their claims are made.

Judith functions as 'the door to the house of the living' (p. 76) for Adam Constant, revealing to him the true meaning of fellow feeling. He seems to awaken her in a similar way but while he burns with plans to publish his poetry and go to China to work with the revolution there, she can look forward to nothing more than being 'the perfect wife' (p. 74) to Jean Frère. Early manuscript drafts show much more of Judith's response to Adam, including a poem entitled 'Judith's Sorrows for Adam Constant' and a fragment depicting Judith's guilt and fear that she will be considered a bad mother when on her return home from an interlude dreaming of Adam she discovers a neighbour comforting her crying child.[3] By cutting these episodes, Stead reinforces the masculine perspectives that silence the feminine in this text. The men see Judith as 'perfect' because she keeps her conflicts to herself. Because Suzanne expresses her frustrations, shakes the bars of her cage, as she puts it, she is seen as a 'gorgon' (p. 490). Judith's fertility finds its opposite in Suzanne, 'the insane goddess of darkness squatting there and dreaming of inchoate things' (p. 490). Their lives, like those of Jules and Carrière, show creativity misdirected and quenched respectively, by the cages in which they find themselves. But unlike the businessmen, they have a humane vision that seeks to change the order of things for the betterment of all rather than to derive profit from it exclusively for themselves. Thus where Jules and Carrière alike are time's subjects, Judith is characterised as 'time-forward' and Suzanne as 'time-abolished' (p. 473). They are the only women shown in the novel to be capable of love (though Judith expresses it creatively and Suzanne destructively). With Jean, Adam and Alphendéry, they are the only characters who act altruistically. Yet these are marginal figures, who appear briefly and disappear before the story's end when Alphendéry abandons them.

The last scene shows Alphendéry saying 'Myself first, the rest nowhere' (p. 785). Jules has disappeared, perhaps to create a new life under a new name. Campoverde has resurrected a new bank on the ashes of the old. Two hundred and eight lawyers are feeding on the fat pastures manured by the bankruptcy. All that energy, all that imagination, all that hate have been expended – and the world continues as it seems it always has. Stead has written what she sees: a drama of waste, betrayal and greed, in which human beings dehumanise themselves and others in exchange for nothing. She leaves the conclusions to be drawn by her readers.

5 Autobiographical Fiction

Stead's move from Europe to the United States marked a shift in her writing from wide-ranging social drama into more closely focused psychological explorations of character. Her next two novels drew more immediately on her personal life, fitting more easily expectations of how a novel should operate and therefore meeting with more enthusiasm from readers. Both are novels of growing up that focus on the female artist as she learns to articulate her own special sense of what it means to be alive in her world.

The Man Who Loved Children: Celebrating the unhappy family

Although the family is the subject of *The Man Who Loved Children*, in the same way that the bank is in *House of All Nations*, one character increasingly absorbs our attention here as no character in a Stead novel has previously. That character is Louisa Pollit, first-born daughter of the man who gives the novel its title, her father Sam. A child verging on adolescence as the novel opens, Louisa grows to maturity through the course of its conflicts to seize her own freedom by the novel's end, where she leaves home to embark on her 'walk round the world'.[1] Louisa is the first Stead heroine who can truly claim to be a female hero. Successfully negotiating the potential traps of home and school, Louisa takes guidance from her selective reading in

literary tradition. She is the 'ugly duckling' (pp. 94 and
487) convinced of her swanhood and determined not to
betray her genius through a failure of nerve. She is also,
like Stead, a 'waker and a dreamer', as her childhood
companion the nightrider makes clear (p. 61).

Children's most striking accomplishment is its portrayal
of the adolescence of a young girl. Surfeited with stories of
male rites of passage, we realise how different (and how
seldom given imaginative form) is the story of the girl's
entry into womanhood. If Joyce's Stephen Daedalus had to
fly past the nets of family, religion and nation, then Louisa
Pollit must negotiate these as well as the more treacherous
webs spun for women in our society. Where Stephen is
from babyhood a voice, Louisa is an ear. Anxiously
drinking in adult conversations trying to make sense of
their mysteries, eavesdropping at doors or compelled to be
audience to her father's endless spiels, she seldom reveals
her own thoughts except on paper. As a child and as a
woman, Louisa learns her survival techniques early. Her
father assumes silence means consent. She seldom bothers
to disabuse him of his mistake. But in her silence she
stages her rebellions, dreams of escape and eventually
invents her own private language to convey all the nuances
of feeling that conventional language obscures. Significantly,
the play that Louisa writes in this language for her father's
birthday is modelled on Shelley's *Cenci* and records a
daughter's destructive and self-destructive hatred of her
father's interference in her life.

The female artist learns to proceed through subterfuge,
identifying her models in male heroes conceived by men
and seeing no irony in that identification. She shapes her
ambitions by reading only about 'men of destiny' (p. 163).
When Sam amends her recitation about the quality most
necessary for the great man to add 'or the woman' (p. 78),
Louisa corrects him stubbornly, 'That is not it'. And
indeed that is not it in her experience. Every detail of her

family life denies her ambitions and insists that woman's role is secondary, to please and serve men. Louisa prepares breakfast and lunch yet when the food is served it is 'Thick for the lads, thin for the girls' (p. 92). When Sam spills a chamber pot, it is the women who must clean up after him and endure his verbal abuse. The children learn their roles leafing through the magazine advertisements with their father, as he rejects or praises the female models according to their looks, saying, 'Not her! She's a fright . . . .' or 'This one's a peacherino . . . young and juicy, a ripe tomato' (p. 65). Louisa knows that by these standards she is a failure. She is clumsy, ugly, badly dressed and sullen. Yet she clings to a belief in herself despite outward appearances, imagining a miraculous transformation will occur if only her will is strong enough.

For Louisa has been sufficiently influenced by the values of her world to imagine herself a theatrical star like Eleanora Duse rather than a writer like Shelley. She takes it for granted that she can hold her brothers and sister spellbound by her stories. She writes plays, poetry and epigrams as naturally as she breathes. But her dreams of escape do not centre on this talent, probably because all the writers she knows are men. Stead distinguishes between Louisa's dreams for her future and her half-brother Ernie's: 'Ernie often thought of making money, but never by putting on a performance himself, say: only by manipulation of objects or of other persons. The idea of selling himself, which was, on the whole, Louisa's idea, of selling her talents on a stage, seemed strange to Ernie' (p. 138). Already, life has taught the eleven-year-old girl that she can only find success by selling herself in one way or another, while the ten-year-old boy knows he will find greater success in manipulating others.

Meanwhile, both must wait to grow up, for they know that to be a child is to be powerless. They feel closer to their mother than to their father because they share this powerlessness with her. After her eleventh birthday, Louisa starts seeing her stepmother as a 'creature of flesh and blood', closer to herself 'because, like the little girl, she was guilty, rebellious, and got chastised' (p. 72). Feminist theory explained how patriarchal culture infantilises women and prolongs childhood in order to maintain its power, but Stead's novel makes that theory clear (at a time when it had not yet been fully elaborated) by showing how it works in practice. Sam is not a villain who consciously oppresses his wife and children in order to prolong his tyranny over them (although Louisa must portray him in such black and white terms in her tragedy in order to reject his influence over her). On the contrary, he is 'the man who loved children' and who worshipped a pure ideal of woman. Stead shows how such 'love' and such 'worship' may prove far more destructive than outright violence, just as liberalism may frustrate genuine change far more effectively than outright opposition. But she also shows that Sam himself is as much the victim as the perpetrator of the ideas he espouses, although his suffering cannot be equated with that of others in the novel for he retains far more power and hence freedom of action than any other character, simply by virtue of his gender and the dominant role it assigns him.

Stead's depiction of personality is so convincing and so powerful that many readers have found themselves drawn into the family battles, either to take sides with Sam against Henny, who they reject as a 'bad mother' or more frequently, at least in recent years, to side with Henny against Sam, who is so smugly self-satisfied in his liberalism that he misses the sexist, racist and even fascist (in his embrace of eugenics) tendencies of his thought. But to take sides in this way is to miss Stead's point. Neither individual is to be blamed. Indeed, it is our conditioned habit to reduce everything to the individual level that Stead is questioning here as in all her work. The feminist slogan that 'the personal is political' has become a cliché. But this cliché oversimplifies a truth that Stead's work explores in such detail that its meaning lives again whenever we open one of her novels. The institution of marriage and the patriarchal attitudes it supports drive Henny and Sam to behave as they do. While their marriage provides an exaggerated expression of the tensions created by the familial structure, it remains a depiction that most readers recognise as essentially true.

Louisa's experience of family life convinces her that she must kill both her parents to free herself and the other children. It is a testament to Stead's skill that she is able to bring her readers to acquiesce in such a decision, a decision that goes against all the pious tenets of received opinion. While Louisa does not literally kill her parents – Henny takes the opportunity proferred her to commit suicide and Sam escapes – still, the psychological liberation that follows from rejecting their tyranny is an enormous step forward. The Freudian slip implicit in Evie's letter to Sam in Malaya – Dead Dad instead of Dear Dad – is repeated in Sam's stunned repetition of Louisa's words above Henny's corpse, her 'I think she's dead, Dad' becoming 'Dead, Dad, Dead Dad' (p. 506) in Sam's echo. Louisa has moved from begging for her freedom to taking it for herself. With the Mother Hen Henny gone, the old Dad is gone too, for without a wife to command, his power is greatly diminished.

Long before the resurgence of feminist theory in the 1960s, Stead recognised that the family was the central institution responsible for the oppression of women and proceeded to show how that was so. As Juliet Mitchell points out in *Woman's Estate*, women's 'subservience in production is obscured by their assumed dominance in their own world – the family'.[2] This 'assumed dominance', in fact, disguises an actual slavery as *The Man Who Loved Children* demonstrates. Critics such as Randall Jarrell who stress the 'conflict of opposites',[3] particularly of 'male and female principles', do the subtlety of the novel's analysis an injustice. Jarrell's phrases misrepresent an unequal relation based on dominance of the male over the female as an equal relation of equivalence. The novel never makes this mistake. Everywhere Stead makes it clear that Henny and Sam are products of specific educations geared to their class as well as their sex. They are not natural forces. They do not represent the essence of their sexes divorced from their material circumstances. Rather, their behaviour arises from their situation, and that situation gives Sam much more power than Henny, both in and outside the home. The phrases 'conflict of opposites' or 'war of the sexes' suggest an opposition of two equal forces, with each drawing on different spheres of power. *The Man Who Loved Children* shows that this theory of 'separate but equal' provides an inadequate explanation of relations between the sexes in marriage. Just as the title of the book focuses on Sam, so does the entire organisation of the family, including Henny's and the children's ineffective revolts against his domination.

The first page of the novel makes Henny's legalised subordination clear when she receives a letter addressed to 'Mrs Samuel Clemens Pollit'. Even her name is not her own. The 'dear little rigmaroles' (p. 43) of her games with the children could occur only 'when Daddy was out'. The language describing her marriage combines imagery of disease with that of imprisonment (p. 45). For Henny, marriage is 'living cancers of insult, leprosies of disillusion, abscesses of grudge, gangrene of nevermore'. Marriage is drudgery, worry and repression. All the work of maintaining the house, feeding and clothing the children, washing and mending, remains invisible to Sam but gradually emerges for the reader, who sees Henny struggling alone with the bills, stuffing mattresses to save money and above all cleaning up after all Sam's messy little projects. When Sam decides to reorganise household tasks along the lines of masculine efficiency, he has the children wash the dishes sloppily and hides the dirty pots, saying the women can do them later. Patriarchal society is run on just such a system of men taking credit for unacknowledged female labour.

But this denial of her achievements has its effects on Henny, too. Her education has prepared her neither to earn money outside the home nor to maintain the home efficiently but merely to aspire to the almost unattainable bourgeois dream of the wife as ornament. 'Water-colour-painting, embroidery, and the playing of Chopin' are all so ludicrously inappropriate for the life of grinding poverty in which she finds herself, that she too comes to share society's opinion that she is worthless. And more than this, she finds herself incapable of imagining an alternative for her children. The narrator comments:

> About the girls she only thought of marriage, and about marriage she thought as an ignorant, dissatisfied, but helpless slave did of slavery. She thought the boys would get on by the brutal methods of men. (p. 458)

Several feminist theorists draw similar analogies between women's oppression and slavery: both systems depend for their dominance on convincing the oppressed of their own inherent inferiority to justify the supposed 'naturalness' of their continuing oppression. Henny's inability to stay within Sam's limited budget while caring for his rapidly increasing family convinces her that she is a failure. She has been bred to be a bad money manager – and she is. Her daughter Evie, whose favourite game is playing Mommy, has already internalised the same lessons but Louisa escapes through her reading, which opens her eyes to the possibility of other ways of living.

In her relationship with her stepmother, Louisa rewrites the fairy tale of Snow White from a radically subversive angle of vision. As Gilbert and Gubar have demonstrated, this story is central to our culture's socialisation of women.[4] Like Snow White, Louisa appears to have an evil stepmother who dislikes her. But Louisa's story reveals that the apparent opposition of stepmother and child conceals a fundamental affinity. Louisa's stepmother Henny sees in the child another woman destined to entrapment through her sex and so lashes out against her own fate in lashing out against Louisa. Smarter and stronger than the Snow White of the fairy tales, Louisa understands this complex identification, sympathises with Henny and determines to escape the trap. By the end she is ready to say, without emotion, 'I am my own mother' (p. 521). She creates herself in defiance of external definitions of what she can be, but especially to reject her father's insistence that she is an extension of himself.

Feminist theorists speculate that the bourgeois family evolved to ensure men's immortality through their children, whom they viewed as both their property and extensions of themselves. Louisa rejects Sam's attempts to claim these male rights through her. Like contemporary feminists, she turns to history to prove that this kind of family is a modern development rather than an unalterable natural occurrence and therefore may be changed. Sam's snooping uncovers a sentence written in her diary in ungrammatical French, which says that 'In the Middle Ages parents sent (their) children to (into the care of) strangers' (p. 369). At the end of the novel, Louisa sends herself into such care, believing it preferable to the incestuous and turbulent demands of the nuclear family.

The taboo against incest, which Freud saw as the basis of civilisation, has always interested Stead. She explored its sexual dimensions in 'The Triskelion' and its psychology in *Seven Poor Men of Sydney*. In *The Man Who Loved Children* she shows it to be integral to twentieth-century family life. Louisa's immediate recognition of her own situation in Shelley's *Cenci*, Sam's promise to Evie, his 'Little-Womey', that she can be his wife, and Sam's unreasonable rage at the punishment of a neighbouring father for the impregnation of his young daughter, all indicate the unacknowledged but powerful undercurrents of repressed sexuality that contribute to family tensions and that prevent the realisation of full human potential. The books Sam gives Louisa to teach her about sexuality reveal the inability of liberal patriarchy to deal with this fundamental human reality. Because he can only conceive of sex as a hideous form of violence against women, he gives her books documenting sexual atrocities committed during war to initiate her into the facts of life as he sees them.

Both parents feel they have been trapped in their marriage through the betrayal of their bodies; Sam through physical desire and Henny through pregnancies. But the horrible stories of the birth of Bonnie's illegitimate child and of their poor neighbour, Mrs Kydd, whose husband John 'beat her, starved her, and insulted her' (p. 110) reveal the special vulnerability of women, whether married or single, in a man's world. As Ernie recognises, access to money provides the only escape from such dismal alternatives. 'Auntie Jo was neither a married woman nor an old maid, nor a schoolma'am, she was a landlord' (p. 137). But to attain such power, she has sacrificed her humanity, turning herself into an asexual, selfish monster. Louisa and her friend Clare want everything: financial independence and sensual gratification.

The novel shows the models they reject. Each is a 'female Caliban' (p. 349); Sam, the Prospero who on his return from Malaya discovers his wand is broken (p. 270), his power over his children dissipated. Sam represents the naive self-confidence of Western civilisation that it has created the best of all possible worlds. Henny's cynicism is merely the other side of his idealism; she cannot imagine an alternative way of arranging human relations. But Clare is exploring socialist theory and Louisa romantic literature in search of radical alternatives. Clare, already an orphan, has no need to leave home, but Louisa must find her own path, leaving even her alter ego behind.

Unlike the male artist, Louisa's creativity is not inspired by the opposite sex, but by her own. Because the dominant culture is male, it has determined that even women should see themselves in male terms, so that the female writer addresses her erotic outpourings to a female Muse. The grand conception of the Aiden cycle and Louisa's letters to Clare reveal her search for models in the inappropriate male traditions of the past. Louisa and Clare are 'square pegs in round holes' (p. 93), who in 1936 refused to change themselves to fit the system. But this refusal meant that all their pent-up energies found no approved channels in which to flow. As Stead says, 'Very different from the political girls, the grinds, and the pretty boy-loving girls, Clare and Louisa expended themselves in days of mad fervour about nothing at all' (p. 440). Louisa finds a tentative direction at the end of the novel, turning instinctively away from her father to seek aid from female connections. She visits Clare for moral support, and plans to visit Aunt Jo for money before turning to her mother's family for long-term aid. *The Man Who Loved Children* documents the turning away from patriarchal bonds toward the forging of new female support systems. It delights in the freedom that change entails. Like Del at the end of Alice Munro's *Lives of Girls and Women*, Louisa discovers that the claiming of independence brings an independent point of view, in which the whole world assumes new dimensions. 'Things certainly looked different: they were no longer part of herself but objects that she could freely consider without prejudice' (p. 522).

Louisa is on her way to discovering means of relating to the world beyond those prescribed by the nuclear family.

Stead exposes its contradictions and its failures to satisfy anyone's needs through Louisa's quest to grow up in a world that seeks to prevent her. Why then does she refer to this novel as a 'celebration of unhappy family life'? It is a celebration as much as an attack because for Stead even misdirected vitality remains a sign of life. The struggles of these characters to live creatively, even within the incestuous constraints of the family, affirms the enduring human potential for a more creative release of energies in the future. Just as Stead herself escaped her family to find fulfilment in a different kind of relationship with her husband, so Louisa, in whom she has clearly invested much of herself, rejects conventional solutions in order to seek what will satisfy her. By intensifying her resolve and clarifying her understanding, Louisa's unhappy family life positively aided that search. Neither marriage nor motherhood could ever appear to be a solution for Louisa, who has seen what they did to her stepmother Henny.

But the novel's ending is only the barest of beginnings. Although Louisa strikes out completely on her own, she still remains dependent on the kindness of others for her survival. Yet she has taken the necessary first step. We know she will never turn back the way Elvira Western did after crossing her first bridge and that she will never give up the way Catherine Baguenault did, to leave one repressive institution only in order to enter another. The novel itself seems our proof that Louisa, true to the Nietzschean quotation which inspires her, will use the chaos of her unhappy family life to give birth to her own dancing star (p. 315). The strong artist rejoices in all aspects of life, recording and questioning what she sees but leaving final judgement to her readers.

For Love Alone: The voyage to Cythera

In Stead's fictional world, the voyage to Cythera represents
the fulfilment of desires forbidden by civilisation's repressive
order. It provides the longed-for escape from the solipsistic
hall of mirrors. An active seeking of union with the other,
the journey toward Cythera is the opposite of the paralysed
drifting of the sons of Clovis toward their deaths. In *The
Man Who Loved Children*, Louisa writes to Clare that she
daily makes 'the voyage to Cytherea'; she is mad with her
heart 'which beats too much in the world and falls in love
at every instant with every reflection that glimmers in it'
(p. 439). This exuberance, this passionate engagement with
life, Louisa shares with Teresa Hawkins, the central
character in *For Love Alone*. Teresa tells Jonathan Crow,
the young man with whom she persuades herself she is in
love, that her life is only a passage to our secret desires, 'to
Cytherea'. 'I always think of coral atolls, submarine
volcanoes, the pearl gulfs of the north, a kind of Darwin's
voyage of discovery, as the voyage to Cytherea'.[5] Although
she knows what the term meant for the French aristocrats,
who indulged their passion for the sexual mysteries on the
islands in the Seine, she does not think of 'their old islands'
when she uses the term, but of her own antipodean
environment, in which the voyage no longer means a
temporary escape from civilisation but a quest to invent an
entirely new mode of living in tune with the natural world.

It is a mistake to see her move to England as a rejection
of Australia, then, as many Australian critics have. Rather,
she follows Jonathan where he has gone in order to convert
him to her idea of love as a free and mutual releasing of
creative energies, a vision she has formed through
combining her eccentric reading with her experience of the
Australian sun and sea. Her understanding of passion owes
much to her reading of a fictional magazine based on the
Lindsays' *Vision*, with its cult of vitalism and its belief in

the antique purity of Australia as a revitalising counter to the decadent modernism coming from Europe. Like Jack Lindsay, the magazine's founder, Stead moved from this apolitical celebration of positive instincts to a political engagement informed by Marxism when she moved, as he did, from Sydney to London.[6] But where the early Lindsay of *Vision* portrayed women as the objects of men's pleasures, Teresa's love is subversive, even revolutionary, because egalitarian and unlimited. It is genuinely free, not the travesty of freedom labelled 'free love' that Jonathan tries to palm off on her as a new excuse for the old exploitation. A modern Saint Teresa, she attempts to convert Jonathan to her secular vision of love as all-encompassing, the source of all joy and creativity in the world, through a self-induced martyrdom that he is incapable of understanding. The language of sainthood is used explicitly throughout the novel in describing Teresa's dedication to her ideal. She makes a 'cult' of Johnny in the same way men have made cults of the Virgin Mary or the 'Cruel Mistress' of courtly love fantasies. In this scenario, the male, rather than the female, is cast as the great withholder of love. He becomes the passive object of the chase. Woman is the hunter stalking her prey. *For Love Alone* turns romantic conventions upside-down, rewriting them from an antipodean point of view – the woman's rather than the man's.

The Man Who Loved Children focuses on the need to escape from an intolerably claustrophobic world in which freedom is impossible. *For Love Alone* turns that need to escape into an active quest for fulfilment. The title, not Stead's own choice, is unfortunate. It suggests the kind of false romanticism all of Stead's work is designed to discredit. In our culture, 'love' has become a silly word, so imprecise as to be almost meaningless. Teresa recognises the inadequacy of our language in conveying the precision of our feelings in one of her letters to Jonathan. She seems to be speaking for Stead when she writes:

All the ecstasies are things within for which there is no
name and which have never been described. The greatest
sensations become the most general and the least
concerned with that particular adjusted interlocking
which is any kind of relation to the outside world . . . .
Language is simply not large enough and although
English is said to have the most synonyms and the most
words altogether, it still lacks hundreds of thousands of
words. That is why love stories I suppose sound so dull,
for the heroine or hero cannot feel just love, it must be
one of a hundred kinds of love he feels. (p. 253)

Despite its title, *For Love Alone* is not a love story in our
normal use of the term, though it is a story about a young
woman who loves life, and who seeks to express that love
through a series of learned gestures: through creative
expression, through ascetic repression, through single-
minded devotion to a man, through sexual love, through
sharing ideas. Her 'love' involves her in dialogue with
three men who profess different perspectives on the subject:
the sadistic Jonathan Crow, the sociable James Quick and
the enigmatic Harry Girton.

Teresa's strenuous idealism often makes her ridiculous
in the eyes of the world. As the novel's epigram suggests,
she is a female Don Quixote, embarked on a 'buffoon
Odyssey' (p. 348) in search of what most people believe to
be unattainable – real personal fulfilment through full
stature as a human being. For the misogynist world in
which she lives, her gender makes her quest even more
comic. Certainly it involves her in apparent contradictions.
Although she is really looking for herself, she appears to be
looking for a man, because conventional wisdom has it that
a woman can only find herself through a man. Thus she
arbitrarily adopts Jonathan as a means toward her end, but
for a time confuses the means with the end. The language
in which she thinks reveals her confusion: 'all other things

were secondary to the need to leave the lonely state that galled and humiliated her as woman and free-man' (p. 224). This is the double bind in which she is caught. 'As woman and free-man' she finds being single humiliating, but the stories of all the married women she hears make it clear that marriage provides no solution. It is simply not possible to be both 'woman and free-man' in her society. It is the most basic contradiction in terms.

Similarly, she sees herself as a medieval knight courting a cruel mistress, feeling that 'she was behaving as behaves a gallant and a brave man who passes through the ordeals of hope deferred, patience, and painful longing, to win a wife' (p. 250). But where such activity may be admirable in a man, in a woman it is perceived as immodest, even foolish, because the man still holds all the power in this romantic game. Teresa is frightening because she takes her society at its word, insisting on claiming the rights it says are hers but knows are not. Her intensity confuses, and flatters as it repels, the cynical Jonathan. Far from seeing her as she sees herself – as a noble, free knight battling fate to win honour – he sees her as a biological reject, a 'sorry sister', so desperate for a man she'll take any punishment.

Their relationship is a comedy of misunderstandings, in which each interprets the other according to his or her own needs and desires. Their poverty appears to unite them. Teresa and Jonathan, the hawk and crow their last names imply, are both hungry birds of prey, seeking sustenance in a world that depends for its survival in its present form on their continuing hunger. Whereas Jonathan has resolved to make his living as a scavenger, preying on those less fortunate than himself – the maids, waitresses, prostitutes and abandoned wives he pretends to befriend – Teresa attempts to soar above all that misery, to live in a headier sphere where she can ignore the sordid 'facts of life'. By the novel's end, each has settled for a private solution, an opting out of the struggle for change, which is why Teresa sighs, 'It's dreadful to think that it will go on being repeated for ever, he – and me! What's there to stop it?' (p. 502). As long as the system survives that has socialised them to behave as they do – he sadistically, she masochistically – there is nothing to stop their experiences being repeated by each new generation of men and women.

In Quick she finds a man willing to grow with her, but still constrained by the inherited values of centuries. When she tries to tell him of her feelings, he goes cold, just as Oliver did when Elvira spoke freely to him in *The Beauties and Furies*. There are a thousand sides to her love, but he wants only 'a woman's love, the intensely passionate, ideal, romantic love of famous love affairs' (p. 459). Although they educate each other slowly towards a freer understanding of their relationship, the happiness they find together is only a private solution to a communal problem that will not disappear until social relations themselves are changed.

The novel both recognises and shies away from this truth. Stead's honesty insists on revealing the dissatisfactions of even the happiest of unions, yet her extreme individualism leads her to distrust the possibility of any political action for change that might make these conditions disappear. Teresa, who refuses to join a union or to confide in another woman, is closely modelled on Stead herself. She can analyse how oppression operates from her own experience, but is not interested in why it exists or how it might be changed, only in finding an escape hatch for herself. For example, Teresa thinks: 'Where we have passions that are uncontrollable as in sex, a difficult social web is conciously spun out of them, with the help of oppressor and oppressed, so that practically no joy may be obtained from them . . . . By "they", I don't know who I mean. But I am trying to get by them – whoever they are' (pp. 254–55). How these oppressions operate – and how people circumvent them – are Stead's chosen subjects: the 'difficult social web' as it enfolds us, not how it might be rent apart or lifted.

Some aspects of this oppressive social web in *For Love Alone* may seem dated today, but it is depressing how few these are. The more blatant inequities may have disappeared, but the principles on which they are based continue to operate. Female schoolteachers no longer need to pledge not to marry but women still earn far less than men for equal work. Today Miss Haviland might not be denied the travelling scholarship she earned on the grounds that she might marry, but the educational system still discriminates against women in other ways. Teresa's struggle for self-determination occurs in an environment in which everything is loaded against her, including the training of her own instincts from birth.

The first few chapters of *For Love Alone* dramatise the complex conditioning process to which women were subjected in the 1930s. The father ranting about selfless love as his daughters slave over the household chores, serving him, provides a perfect image of the contrast between how society speaks of women in ideal terms while treating them as unpaid servants. The double standard the father imposes on them, demanding that they be 'womanly' and please men without resorting to 'feminine wiles', cannot possibly be met. Neither Kitty with her submissive adoption of the traditional feminine role of housewife nor Teresa with her proud independence can meet their father's impossible demands. Kitty is criticised for not earning money and Teresa for being too cold. Similarly, women are despised if they remain unmarried and despised for chasing men to 'entrap' them in marriage. Their supposed tendency to marry is used to justify their exclusion from education, work and decent pay, but when this exclusion forces them into marriage they are accused of marrying a meal ticket. Yet the father remains head of the household despite the fact that he himself has not worked in years!

Teresa's extreme naiveté about sex enables her to remain unaware of how thorough a disadvantage her gender is. She simply does not understand her father's sniggering remark that a woman's honour is something quite different from a man's (p. 13), just as she cannot imagine what danger there might be for her in walking about and sleeping alone in the countryside. Most of her sufferings come from her ignorance. The novel is intensely critical of an educational system that meets the needs of no one. Through its puritanism, it prolongs the adolescence of girls like Teresa. Through its elitism, it gives her cousin Ellen false ideas of gentility that isolate her from her social class while providing her with nothing in return. It encourages the mediocrity and viciousness of Jonathan; and it rejects those genuinely eager for knowledge like Miss Haviland. In short, it functions only to maintain the inequitable class system, as Teresa's so-called 'mad class' makes clear. Teresa's rejection of her job as a schoolteacher, then, becomes a symbolic rejection of the indoctrination and conformity of the educational system. She does not know who 'they' are, but she knows they work through the schools, and she wants no part of that work.

But the novel focuses more attention on Teresa's private life than on her work as a teacher or her new work as a secretary. Although Teresa enjoys her work she has been raised to think her real life must be elsewhere – in relation to a man. This artificial separation between public and private breaks down, however, when her boss, James Quick, finds himself in love with her. Her role as 'office wife' leads easily into her role as 'backstreet wife'. (Erskine's earlier courtship of her, which now looks very much like what we would call sexual harassment, shows how vulnerable the woman is even at work.) Teresa is flattered, but not really moved, by this succession of men who seem always to be grabbing and kissing her. Her refusal to recognise their economic power over her enables her to maintain a sense of her own integrity. She does not recognise the laws of the marketplace, but makes her own rules, believing that 'everything in the world was produced by the act of love' (p. 110), not by economic necessity.

Stead's focus on sexuality as the chief arena in which the battle for equality must be waged was taken up by many feminist writers in the sixties and seventies. Emotional independence must accompany financial independence, but not, as with Jonathan, at the expense of our humanity. *For Love Alone* charts one woman's painful journey toward the winning of an emotional independence that includes and expands, rather than denies, her ability to love. Teresa always wanted more than the long 'marriage-sleep' of the suburbs. With Quick, she finds a partner open enough to allow their marriage (itself a de facto one since Quick is already legally married to someone else) to be not a sleep but a continual series of awakenings.

From her affair with Girton, she brings back a greater love to Quick and a new utopian vision of the potential of all humanity to continue striving toward the good: 'there was something on the citied plain for all of them' (p. 494). Teresa's experience proves that the traditional wisdom of 'old wive's tale' and 'father's admonition' (p. 495) can be questioned and must be questioned if we are to find a way of realising instead of wasting the energies that are ours. The extreme deprivation of her adolescence is mirrored in the stories of produce dumped at sea while the people starve; the hope of her new life with Quick, whose name signifies life, is on the contrary that 'all pleasures, all desires should be for all' (p. 494). For plenty to replace want requires a turning upside-down of our entire inheritance from the past. We must try to look at everything again, with fresh eyes unclouded by prejudice. The alternative is the 'self-pickled' (p. 500) misery of Crow.

Stead, then, makes a number of daring innovations in *For Love Alone*. She portrays the sexual fantasies of the adolescent girl with an honesty and vividness that is quite unusual. She then shows how this fertile energy is humiliated, deprived, finally driven underground and twisted, not just in Teresa's story, but in her cousins Anne, Malfi and Ellen's lives too, in her sister Kitty's and in her friend Miss Haviland's. The entire novel is a powerful refutation of Jonathan's misogynist essay on female sexuality. Teresa's story is meant to be emblematic. In Quick's mind, 'the tragedy, embroilment, and heedlessness of everyone became mixed with the fate of Teresa Hawkins alone' (p. 396). Her fight against the degrading prejudices of Jonathan's mélange of racist, sexist and facist slogans is humanity's fight to free itself from the 'dark plain' of misery these prejudices maintain. As in all her books, Stead asks, here through Teresa: 'If nothing that is, suits people, why do they all take it lying down? Because they have so little time, no money – but is that enough excuse?' (p. 75). *For Love Alone* answers no. It seeks to show how capitulation is inevitably self-defeating. Our only way out is through open rebellion.

These autobiographical fictions affirm that change is possible. We are not trapped by biology or society – only by ourselves. The dice may be loaded against women and children but they can escape defeat simply by refusing to play by the rules of the game. To read these novels is to feel exhilarated by the energy they release. Far from underestimating the forces working against change, they record them in such pitiless detail that the triumphs when they come are undeniably earned.

According to Stead, the most decisive moments in both novels record imaginative departures from the facts of her own life. Louisa's poisoning of her mother's tea and her leaving home at fifteen, and Teresa's affair with Girton, provide dramatic resolutions to problems not so easily resolved in Stead's own life. Two conclusions may be drawn from this observation. Both are important for understanding the direction of Stead's later work. Firstly, life seldom conforms to the tidy patterns encouraged by conventional fictional structures. Secondly, the psychological fears of change may have been underestimated by Stead in her depictions of Louisa and Teresa. Stead is very hasty in her denials of a factual basis in her own life for the Girton affair, while admitting the temptation existed.[7] A posthumously published autobiographical story recreates the same characters and dynamics of attraction but this time shows the heroine resisting the temptation to follow her desires, choosing instead to maintain the equilibrium of her marriage.[8] The problem of sexual attractions beyond marriage interested Stead, and it is crucial to the feminism of *For Love Alone*. If Stead was telling the truth in her interviews, she made an imaginative leap in the novel that she was not prepared to make in her own life, allowing Teresa full development as a human being while denying that freedom to herself. Imaginatively she could see that Teresa's moving beyond the conventional limitations of marriage could enhance the genuine love she shared with Quick but at the same time she feared the implications of such a challenging of social givens in her own life. Whether this reading is correct or not, in the novels after *For Love Alone* Stead turned away from utopian projections of the realisation of desires, symbolised for her in the voyage to Cythera, to closer considerations of the tendencies in human nature, encouraged by our present social structures and habits of thought, that lead people to abandon Cythera for less satisfying alternatives.

6 American Dreams

In the prewar period that inspired Stead's earlier fiction and during the Second World War when *The Man Who Loved Children* and *For Love Alone* appeared, things looked so bleak that real structural changes in the organising of society seemed possible. But the direction events took in the postwar period dashed such hopes. For American frequenters of radical circles like Stead's friends and like her next heroine Letty Fox, this period could best be described as a 'moral bottom'.[1] Their dreams had to be scratched or rethought from the bottom up. Whereas *The Man Who Loved Children* confidently challenged the American dream of the affluent nuclear family, *Letty Fox* and the American novels that followed it consider the tenacity of such myths. Despite their failure, people clung to them. So Stead's novels returned to their Depression preoccupations with the power of dreams to obscure reality, leading people to mistake their own best interests or to give up hope of anything better.

Letty Fox: Her Luck: Beyond Cythera

Louisa Pollit believes in her genius; Teresa Hawkins in her fate. Letty Fox's motivating belief is in her luck. Luck leads her a merry dance but gives her what she thinks she wants in the end. The problem is that wishes once granted have a way of turning out differently than the wisher imagined. This is the point of the joke Letty repeats about the king who asked the fairy to make him like his horse – without first checking the state of his horse. Emasculation seems to be an underriding fear in the circles Letty frequents; and no wonder, for to be like a woman in this society is to be powerless indeed.

In her introduction to the Angus and Robertson reprint Meaghan Morris suggests that '*Letty Fox* is remarkable in being one of the few radical novels about why a woman might want to opt in.'[2] Letty's generation takes the sexual freedom Teresa's struggled for as if it were a natural right. Letty enjoys it but since it comes unaccompanied by other freedoms – either economic or emotional – the pressures to 'voluntarily' abandon it in favour of marriage are too great to resist. The chief interest of *Letty Fox* for our generation is the way it presents the transition from the hard-won victories of Teresa's age to what Letty calls 'the moral bottom' of the fifties.

The serious high-minded idealism of Louisa and Teresa would have been inappropriate to such a task. If naiveté plagued the undereducated women of the earlier years of this century, a false precocity seemed to characterise the young American girls Stead observed during the forties in the United States. In some ways *Letty Fox* marks the sharpest break yet in Stead's writing career. After the two autobiographical novels, she moves on to depict a character with a background and goals completely removed from her own and for the first time in her work to allow that character to speak the entire novel in her own voice, stamping it with her own individual personality.

Yet Letty's concerns are Teresa's concerns: nationality, class and temperament may separate them but gender unites them. Letty too confronts the problems of women's socialisation, the gap between official moralities and practice, the choice which is no choice between marriage and remaining single. But she confronts them from a radically different perspective, that of the sexually liberated young woman of the world. Her racy style is a relief after Teresa's naiveté. In itself it challenges many current myths about how a woman should think and act. But what she describes in that style is a world of limited opportunities, of external and internal oppressions so pervasive as to leave very little room for individual manoeuvring. Letty says bluntly:

> In other times, society regarded us as cattle or handsome house slaves; the ability to sell ourselves in any way we like is a step towards freedom; we are in just the same situation as our Negro compatriots – and they would not go backwards towards their miserable past. One must take the good with the bad and, unmoved by the titles of things and worn-out prejudice, one must look towards the future. (p. 5)

Letty's iconoclasm combines pragmatism with hope. Speculating on the failure of all her love affairs, Letty echoes Virginia Woolf in her conclusion that 'a room of my own was what I principally lacked' (p. 4). Letty too is a writer but without an independent income. For Letty, therefore, the requisite room of one's own still means independence but not as envisioned by Woolf. Far from providing the privacy necessary to writing, it provides her with a necessary edge in marketing herself to men in her quest to join organised society through marriage.

This 500-page novel relates the details of that quest. Letty's book begins with her finding a room of her own and starting to write the story of her life. She explains her approach: 'I reckoned I knew enough about life to write a real book of a girl's life. Men don't like to think that we are just as they are. But we are much as they are . . . .' (p. 11). A modern Moll Flanders, Letty is unrepentant about the methods used to attain her goal: 'I was not always honest, but I had grit, pretty much; what else is there to it?' (p. 502). To launch herself in life an unmoneyed woman requires enterprise. Letty is not a complainer but her story makes it clear that she is playing a game in which the dice are loaded against her. She inhabits a world where a woman's wit and intelligence are perceived as an essential part of the sexual packaging of the product. They do not make her any less of a sexual commodity; they merely increase her value on the market. And in New York it is a very competitive market. Energetic, funny, precocious as she is, Letty does not see herself as particularly special. Indeed, until Bill van Week marries her, she thinks of herself as a failure. Although Letty works for a living and proves herself an exceptionally good worker, she remains chiefly sexual prey to her bosses, gaining promotion when she is in favour and finding the job unbearable when she inevitably loses their favour. Such conditions make the building of a serious career extremely difficult. In comparison, marriage appears the easier option.

Yet in the face of her society's constant devaluation of her personhood and of her work, Letty retains her own sharp point of view. She is irrepressible. Without being consciously feminist, Letty refuses to see herself as in any way unequal to men. By virtue of the way society is organised, the men she wants have greater earning power than she does and this gives them the upper hand in negotiating emotional relationships. Always the pragmatist, she recognises this imbalance of power and does her best to circumvent it. She tries to buy Clays but must bow to the superior economic capacity of the Honourable Fysshe. She senses that her '*homme fatal*' (p. 359), Luke, could be bought but again she simply cannot afford him. Bill she considers 'the best bargain I could have got out of life' (p. 498) and the baby she is carrying a dividend for the future, the beginning of her own capital. Her pregnancy enables her to understand 'why society is organised in ways that seem strange to youngsters. It is, of course, organised to a certain extent for babies' (p. 499). These insights, common to feminist analyses of the seventies, emerge casually, through the action of this novel first published in 1946, in a period when literature and the media were persuading women to abandon the workforce for the home.

Letty's apparent acceptance of such propaganda – as the best she can do out of a world not organised around her needs – while refusing to believe it true – provides a far more convincing feminist statement than outright rejection. By the novel's end, Letty hopes she has found what she has been looking for in her pregnancy but is careful not to ask herself whether this feeling will last. She is more inclined to share her father's mistress Persia's debunking of the mythology of motherhood (p. 154) than to believe in it herself. After all pregnancy did not save her mother Mathilde's marriage nor did it satisfy her frustrated career desires. Of her mother, Letty said: 'She had acquired all the advertised products, love, a husband, a home, children, but she had not the advertised results – she recognized nothing in the landscape' (p. 75). Letty begins with fewer illusions. Bill has been married twice already and her description of his charms is the kind of catalogue of physical features one is more accustomed to find in descriptions of beauty queens than of husbands. In Letty's book what is sauce for the goose is sauce for the gander. She can see already that Bill's 'pleasant blue eyes' are 'perhaps at times a little empty' (p. 498) but what does that matter when the Fox has captured herself a Week? (A short period of time as a breathing space and perhaps also a weak man, one she can manage.) Unlike her mother, she does not expect the 'advertised results' but merely hopes to get through life with some self-respect. In the world Letty describes this in itself is a heroic goal.

Letty retains her self-respect by refusing to let the importance of money dominate her life. She is looking for the truth about herself, for a way to remain alive into middle age and beyond. Like Teresa she wants something better than the marriages she sees around her but unlike Teresa she cannot believe in the saving power of 'a great love'. She sees her sister Jacky's idealism as hopelessly foolish, if enviably passionate. She herself concentrates on continuing the battle to avoid being eaten (pp. 165–66). She knows that 'you have to keep on fighting for liberty, even in a revolution when you're on the right side'. And she knows too that 'this is more than most people can bear' (p. 383). But she's a battler. She can bear it. And she keeps on fighting – in the fox's way. Making Napoleon's motto hers – '*On s'engage et puis on voit*' – she loves life and exposes herself to it (p. 502). Thus she can say that she 'wonders at the simplicity' of people who think love affairs bad for a woman. 'As for men – I don't answer for them. Men are easily debauched because they think of every woman they have had as a conquest, although it is clear that it is a mutual conquest and that each loses what each gains' (p. 6). This philosophy of love stands her in good stead. Unlike her mother, she never sees herself as a victim. She makes lasting friends of her lovers. She retains her integrity.

Letty's love of life spills out naturally into her political speeches and her creative writing as well as her numerous love affairs. It is surprising to find most critical commentary taking Letty at her word to see her as an ordinary girl looking for a man to marry her. Yet by the age of 24 she has produced far more than either Louisa or Teresa, who are always discussed as emerging artists. Their seriousness seems to warrant their claims to artistry, while Letty's flippancy seems to discount hers. Yet when we remember that Stead herself hated to think of herself as a professional writer, insisting that she did not have a career but was merely a person who wrote, we may want to look more closely at Letty, who is also modest about her writing but who nonetheless writes continually and has presumably written the story of her life we are now reading. Edwige Lantar is the professional writer in this book. Her novel, callously written to commercial specifications with smut on every page, proves the best seller she planned it to be. Edwige is the true immoralist, because she cannot understand that there is 'any pleasure in creation' (p. 162) or any value beyond getting ahead materially. Letty, in contrast, wants 'to be truthful' (p. 165), believes there is more to life than Edwige's ugly world of cut-throat self-interest and writes for the pleasure of creating. She makes fun of her own adolescent efforts to write 'the great American novel of the youth of 1936' (p. 226) – yet that is exactly what she has done in *Letty Fox: Her Luck*.

Letty's picaresque adventures span the period between her birth in 1921 to her marriage in 1945. She lives through the Depression, the Spanish Civil War and the Second World War and is preparing to enter the somnolence of the postwar period when her story closes. Her life exemplifies the maturing of America and its changing social mores. The novel is encyclopaedic in its commentary on education, psychiatry and male/female relationships in the new Republic. In addition, it contains in embryo the plots of the two slighter American novels which followed it: Cornelis de Groot's infatuation with his avaricious mistress exactly parallels Robbie Grant's ensnarement by the blondine in *A Little Tea, a Little Chat*, and the Morgan family's empire seems a bawdier version of the gentle Massines of *The People with the Dogs*, which delineates in more detail the postwar world of unemployment, crowded housing and the new conservatism.

Like Edward Massine, Letty loves New York. It is her home; she knows it intimately through years of walking everywhere and visiting friends in bars. Strange men following her or pinching and fondling her on the subway, are minor harassments she has learned to live with because they have always been 'the custom of the town'. After the war, however, she finds her freedom much curtailed by an increased violence against women. Letty suddenly finds herself excluded from many of her old haunts, as 'a lot of town became impossible' (p. 462). One night, as she is sitting in a place she had known for years with an old schoolfriend, now a doctor, the two women find themselves abused by two ex-soldiers. When their advances are rejected, the men sneer, 'Then what are you here for?' (p. 463). Letty is furious but also embarrassed by this assault on her selfhood and this denial of her freedom. The incident reveals to her 'the great shame in which we all lived'. She feels 'blue' for a week but after a few similar incidents, sharpens her tongue, preparing to battle on while protecting Jacky from the worst of it.

Stead's greatness emerges most clearly in scenes like this. Every woman can recognise its truth but how seldom such everyday experiences make it into the literature we have been taught to view as 'universal'. Stead's realism delineates the subtle links between the harassing of two women in a bar and the pent-up violences released by the Second World War and by the oppressive relation between the sexes in a manner so intimately a part of her narrative that many readers still miss the fact that there is analysis here at all. Because she fails to meet the traditional expectations of both male and female readers, being neither emotional nor polemical, she has been dismissed as a naive realist. Nothing could be further from the case. Letty appears to ramble on but always for a purpose. As she writes to Clays: 'there'll be no sense in sexual theories until women start telling their minds; and, of course, until they have some; that'll be when they abolish the ads . . . .' (p. 258).

Letty presents herself as a transitional generation between the great tribe of Morgan women who live through parasitical marriages and alimony and that represented by her younger sister Andrea and her friend Anita, who want to work and have babies but see no need for marriage. Whereas the earlier generation, slaves to what the popular magazines told them, became instantly incapacitated with the advent of motherhood, believing all happiness must be sacrificed to the child, these girls take motherhood in their stride, refusing to change their pleasure-seeking habits. Grandmother Morgan's philosophy never worked for more than a few. She had claimed:

> The men marry us, keep us and our children; give us allowances, buy life insurance, and leave us their money and even hand us alimony! But all for one reason, and one reason alone. To buy us off! They don't want us running the world; they are willing to pay a lot, so they can run it themselves. It's insurance, as I see it. (p. 251)

Increasingly, however, the men refuse to pay this insurance, some like Uncle Percy Hogg and Uncle Philip even preferring jail before choosing exile and suicide respectively rather than face their vengeful women. Finally, with the increasing disproportion between the numbers of men in relation to women after the mass slaughter of two world wars, the system breaks down completely. There are too many women to buy them all off and the men are no longer willing to pay the price. *Letty Fox* portrays the gap between the official ideology, linking love and marriage, and the cynical observations of the actual social order made by Grandmother on the one hand and by Letty's father on the other. He suggests that if we looked at our own society with the objective eye of the anthropologist – one of Stead's favourite images for shifting perspectives – we would describe it as polygamous. Yet monogamy remains the official ideal. The tension between the two bothers Letty. Although naturally and happily polygamous herself, she wants marriage with one man in order to gain social acceptance, even though she knows how foolish this goal is and envies Anita her freedom from it.

The debates between Jacky and Letty bring together the idealistic worship of life that characterised Louisa and Teresa in the earlier two novels (here embodied in Jacky) with a satirical intelligence (here Letty's) that was always there but never fully embodied in a fictional character before. Letty puts it this way: 'She saw how things ought to be, I saw how things must be' (p. 43). Yet it is also true that Letty is a socialist who finds the present order unsatisfactory while Jacky is a conservative who sees no need for revolution. *Letty Fox* marks the point in Stead's work where she turned increasingly toward Letty's kind of seeing although the two are always coexistent in her work. Both the idealist and the materialist perspectives have their place. Stead values the strengths and satirises the weaknesses in both positions with an apparent impartiality that continues to confuse those of her critics who wish to discover a simpler ordering of things – one character or one point of view with which to identify.

Both Jacky and Letty are moved to assume their opposed positions by aesthetic impulses. Letty claims: 'I never could stand anything poor, wretched and ugly. If I am a socialist, it is just because of that' (p. 201). Jacky writes: 'Life is really maddeningly *delicious*! All this makes me mad with enthusiasm for things as they are now' (p. 205). Jacky is responding to her discoveries of great literature and art, Letty to the lives of the people around her. Both are part of our lives but neither alone presents the whole picture. Each misrepresents the other's position, Letty sneering that Jacky dislikes Marx because she can't fall in love with him (p. 456) and Jacky pretending to think Letty wants to reduce the world to dull-grey conformity (p. 202). But the novel misrepresents neither of them, including these charges along with other details of their lives to show that nothing is as simple as some of us would like it to be.

That is why Stead crowds her fictions with characters, each
with his or her own point of view, derived from experience:
in Jacky's words, her writing seeks to explain 'the causes of
suffering and love' (p. 203) in all their complexity.

Letty Fox makes fun of all attempts to reduce this
complexity to a formula: the Questions and Answers of
Amy, the 'baby Chesterfield' (p. 390); Letty's own
advertising slogans; the pat Freudian con game of the
psychiatrist Letty's 'perfect American male' persuades her
to visit. This psychiatrist tells her 'a father fixation'
prevents her from marrying; she thinks it more likely the
war has something to do with it. He tells her the only way
out is through analysis; Persia suggests she would be better
off with a fortune-teller (pp. 466–67).

In *Letty Fox*, Stead for the first time portrays the full
education of a woman from childhood to maturity. Because
Letty is an iconoclastic conformist – tough-minded,
worldly wise and a 'generous fool' who knows her Marxian
theory – she proves the ideal instrument for revealing the
follies of her times. As a spoiled, bratty child who knows
exactly how to manipulate her parents, she satirises
Mathilde's reliance on pseudo-psychological women's
magazines for the formulas which will make her children
complex-free and bring her husband back to her. As a
young adult, she lectures her friend Susannah for a similar
fetishisation of Freud American-style – that is bowdlerised
to suit the prejudices of the times.

Through all this comedy, Stead reveals how subtly the
entire organisation of our society – schools, mental health,
advertising and popular culture – are designed to separate
the personal from the political, to discount the links
between our lives and our times, directing us to look
inward rather than outward for an understanding of our
problems. All this false advice Letty Fox debunks. What
she offers instead is a fresh perspective, free of inherited
prejudice, that defamiliarises the world we thought we

knew, enabling us to see it, not as conditioned by a natural order of things but as arbitrarily and inefficiently man-made – and therefore capable of change. Throughout her story Letty has spoken of herself as a ship without a port to steer for. For her, marriage is not the end of her sailing but the beginning. It has provided her with freight and she feels the journey – for her an abandoning of the hopes for unlimited fulfilment promised by Cythera – can begin.

A Little Tea, a Little Chat: The whirligig of values

In *A Little Tea, a Little Chat* Stead records the New York counterpart of the business underworld whose Parisian milieu she explored in *The House of All Nations*. Robbie Grant, *Tea*'s central character, is an Henri Léon without the zest, the humour and the fitful generosity that made Léon, for all his faults, an interesting character. Grant too likes to 'make whoopee' with paid women but more often terms it 'a little tea, a little chat'. The prim euphemism sums up the tenor of his vicious yet boring life. Just as Léon found himself bested by a smart American blonde, so Robbie, the inveterate lecher, finds himself bested at his own game by the European adventuress he calls 'the blondine'. Her self-possession makes her the only woman he can neither shake nor ruin, earning his admiring appraisal that she is 'more a man than a woman'[3] for a coldness that matches his own. Yet even the blondine merely holds her own. His nemesis arrives in the shape of Hilbertson, a man who unlike Robbie 'still carried in him his passion' (p. 393) and whose enigmatic presence alone is enough to kill Robbie with a heart attack. Robbie, whom we have observed cheating, lying and deceiving himself and others throughout the novel, neither receiving nor giving pleasure in all his transactions, can only meet his fate personified in another, for without an inner life he is incapable of guilt except in the form of fear of another's revenge.

Herein lies the central problem of the novel: how to convey the poverty of the unexamined life that hungers to draw attention to itself but offers nothing to that attention save the endless, repetitive tale of its sinking ever deeper into vice. Stead succeeds in revealing a thoroughly petty, nasty life but she fails in making her readers see why that life demands their attention. There are unrealised hints in the novel that this story was not meant to fall so flat. David Flack and his daughter Edda, decent people, speak of loving Robbie and admiring his genius; this is incomprehensible, given the character as he is written. More puzzling, because more ambitious, are the frequent attempts to link Robbie's affairs to the progress of the Second World War and new developments in American capitalism.

Robbie goes on at tedious length about the story of his life he is offering Edda as the plot for a novel to make her fortune. The novel he imagines contains the same material as *A Little Tea, a Little Chat*, but presented as naive romance rather than sardonic exposure. The only fantasy element is the introduction of a 'dream girl', a woman who will give up fame to come home and cook his breakfast for him. Robbie's version of this classic Hollywood story reiterates the postwar propaganda to get women out of the workforce and back into homes that so depressed Letty at the end of the war but in such a caricatured form that it shows up the formula for the garbage it is. Yet at one point he envisions something less sacharine:

Look, we'll write about the new world, a new world, that is. The U.S.A. has new values, doesn't know how to use them. The old world needs new values U.S.A. has – that will be our theme, not me, see. Of course, you got to have human values too. Look, in Europe they all compounded a felony. They put up with Hitler. The whirligig of values, see. In old times a king threw his serving man out the window, no one would talk to him, they wrote him down in books, called him Pedro the Cruel or something; now, not. Everyone talks to Hitler after Munich . . . . (pp. 46–47)

A Little Tea, a Little Chat is best understood as a study of the 'whirligig of values', written from within that whirl, rather than outside looking down from a distance. This involved perspective accounts for its frenetic yet apparently aimless motion, its rush from one event to another and its failure to distinguish the significant from the trivial.

People put up with Robbie too; and if at first it seems ludicrous to compare this petty businessman to a dictator who caused the deaths of millions, the novel seeks to persuade us that the same social context has produced both of them and that their differences are of degree not kind. As much of the novel is devoted to Robbie's hangers-on as to himself. Stead seeks to understand why people allow themselves to be used by such monsters; how they can attain the power over others that enables them to continue on their destructive ways. Robbie offers nothing but empty promises; yet people are so desperate they will sell themselves for these.

If we think of *A Little Tea, a Little Chat* as a novel of New York during the Second World War, just as we think of *House of All Nations* as a novel of prewar Paris, we will be in a better position to understand the novel than if we see it simply as the story of a seducer seduced. To Robbie, women are only another type of commodity to speculate on as a kind of relief from more serious business: 'Ever since his early manhood, since his marriage, he had bought women; most had been bargains and most had made delivery at once. He never paid in advance: "I got no time for futures in women"' (pp. 55–56). In a heart-to-heart talk with his son Gilbert, he clarifies this relation further: 'Property is a woman, remember . . . . Now I don't say woman to mean woman. A woman with property acts like a man. In property there are no sexes . . . . In property, anyone who wins is right' (pp. 344–45). Robbie, like Stead's more attractive characters, sees 'woman' as essentially a social construct rather than simply a biologically determined being but because he only cares to prey on women, he uses this insight to avoid women who are his economic equals. He takes no pleasure in women themselves, only in his ability to accumulate them cheaply. His sole criterion of value is cost: 'if it's a big love affair I give big pay' (p. 59).

In a confused speech, he compares the blondine to a field of wheat, to adulterated food, to blood gone bad in a blood bank, all once free but now corrupted because only accessible to 'monopolists and gangsters'. 'They can all be allowed to the people only at high prices, and so there's a sort of poison, rust, a rotten dew on that blood and that wheat, and even on my blondine, and so the wheat and cotton is whored' (p. 67). Through these mixed metaphors he seeks to express his intuitive perception that everything becomes tainted when reduced to its monetary exchange value alone. The debased romantic metaphor of the 'dream girl' represents his sense that other values do exist but he fails to act on this dim perception. Instead, he continues to act as a profiteer, even to the extent of welcoming Pearl Harbour and the subsequent declaration of war as 'a golden harvest' (p. 52), during which enormous profits may be made from shipping essential materials to the enemy. Such behaviour is the logical outcome of his placing profits first. He will betray his country in war just as he does his women in love for the higher value of money. Indeed, he sees war as merely another business opportunity. While such observations about the profitability of war have become more common since Vietnam, they were seldom

voiced or understood in America during the period when
this novel appeared.

Unlike Grant, Flack hates and fears money, recognising
that the servants of money want to kill unbelievers like
himself. When he speaks of that hatred his voice becomes
shrill, 'as an honest man seeing the approach of a fascist
policeman who had once tortured him' (p. 361). The
accumulation of such analogies between the trivial affairs
of these characters and the momentous events in Europe
have the effect of compelling us to search for Stead's intent
in drawing them to our attention. Is there an affinity
between the American values espoused by Robbie and
more violently by March on the one hand, and those
advocated by Hitler and Mussolini on the other? Why else
would the blondine describe her blackmailing husband,
ironically – or tellingly – named Churchill, as a Hitler
holding the world to ransom (p. 310)? Why else would
Robbie compare his failure to keep his promises to God's
failure to save His Chosen People from the Nazi gas
chambers (p. 338)? Why else would Stead show Robbie
dreaming of drowning in muddy fields in wartime, sinking
deeper and deeper into the filth with slime filling his eyes,
ears and mouth, and taking this dream as a sign that he is
sinking lower, 'sinking in mud' (p. 375)? Earlier he had
compared the progress of his affair with the blondine to a
'war map, with front lines and back lines and strategic
retreats and lines of communication and hidden depots, of
spies and forces . . .', adding that it was 'even like a
business' (p. 273). This sordid affair, then, seems designed
to mirror both the progress of modern warfare and that of
modern capitalism, presenting them as essentially self-
interested and interdependent games a few powerful men
play with the lives of others.

But such a lacklustre relationship simply cannot carry
such a weight of meaning. The analogies seem tasteless,
even shocking; they fail to convince. *The House of All*

Nations succeeds because each incident reflects on the others and carries a significance in itself. In contrast, most of the action in *A Little Tea, a Little Chat* seems pointless. Because the focus is on Robbie's arid private life, rather than his business deals, he fails to establish either his representativeness or his importance. Indeed, March emerges through his brief appearances, as a far more significant and sinister figure. With his shadowy subjection to the Mafia, his fascist ambitions for a xenophobic, efficient United States, operating 25 hours a day to 'squeeze every last ounce of energy out of it and every last penny of profit' (p. 75), and above all with his vicious abuse of his wife and humiliating subjection to his daughter's whims, he proves a far more convincing embodiment of the 'whirligig of values' than the tedious Robbie. He is responsible for some of the best scenes in the book: the account of Flack's first visit to his country house and of the visit Flack and Robbie pay to the house March is building for the gangsters O'Donovan and Pantalona. Except for the farcical scene in which Gilbert uneasily entertains his mother, Mrs Grant, and his father's two most ambitious mistresses, the blondine and Livy Wright, the rest of the book lacks the tensions so expertly handled here.

A Little Tea, a Little Chat portrays the bland face of evil, showing how liberal humanism disguises vicious exploitation so successfully that even those wielding power can convince themselves they are not responsible for the results of their actions. Robbie is not a hypocrite so much as morally bankrupt. He can believe that 'Negroes should have political equality, though they should not be allowed in uptown restaurants' (p. 15) and feel genuinely offended if someone points out the contradiction implicit in never letting your right hand know what your left hand is doing. Critics such as Lidoff mistake Stead's meaning when they see Robbie and other Stead characters like him as inherently evil. Raised an atheist, Stead believed that traditionally

Christian divisions between good and evil obscured rather than explained what was wrong with our world. The real life character on whom Robbie and Léon were modelled was a friend, yet her artist's eye saw beyond friendship to those elements in contemporary thinking that would continue to thwart real social change. Robbie's incoherent but calculated talk of 'dream girls' and 'Marxist values' shows how the Right managed to pre-empt initiative from the Left at the end of the Second World War and how it has held on to its ascendancy ever since. Unlike Milton, Stead is not of the Devil's party without knowing it. By demonstrating how well-meaning people can support and even initiate actions that hurt others and damage the social fabric, she refuses the easy scapegoating of 'bad' people by the 'good' to show instead that the individual never acts outside a social context which makes certain kinds of action unthinkable. Capitalism makes sexism and fascism seem inevitable. Only if one can imagine an order in which money is no longer the sole determinant of value can one move beyond the 'moral bottom' of *A Little Tea, a Little Chat*. Stead makes moral bankruptcy look boring, unimaginative, ugly and ordinary. But in portraying a world entirely given over to its sway, she risks alienating her readers' attention. Few of us can bear so grim a vision.

The People with the Dogs: The communal dream

The people with the dogs are the Massine family, held together by a grandfather's legacy of a country estate under certain conditions: 'Peace, liberty, a roof for everyone, all claims equal'.[4] Whitehouse, where the family gathers every summer, at first seems to fulfil this dream, creating a closeness and warmth so pleasurable as to be enervating for some, like the 33-year-old Edward, recently returned from service in the Second World War and uncertain what to do with his life. He lives in a state of mind he calls 'undefined hesitant anticipation' (p. 95), too comfortable as he is, living off the rents of his two houses in town, to bother looking for a job, and too happy with friends and family to want to marry his nagging girlfriend of eleven years standing, Margot Rossi. The novel follows Edward as he moves between New York City and Whitehouse (the capitol of economic and cultural dreams and the capitol of political dreams), waiting for something to happen. Eventually, Margot leaves him to marry another man and he falls in love with an actress named Lydia. In marrying her, he realises he must leave much of the old life behind; she will want to travel working in summer stock, not moulder in the country at Whitehouse. At one stroke, she frees him from his family entanglements, provides him with a job in her theatre company, and satisfies his need for someone to love. Although Edward is unhappy about abandoning Whitehouse and the dream it implies, he realises that dream is dead. The novel ends with a St Valentine's Day party celebrating the family's love for one another and Edward's marriage, which is easily embraced by that love.

Like most of Stead's work, this book puzzles over the question of love, but shifts the focus away from the sexual, which predominated in *For Love Alone*, *Letty Fox* and *A Little Tea, a Little Chat*, back to the family orientation of *The Man Who Loved Children*. If Sam loved children, the Massines love dogs. And if *The Man Who Loved Children* celebrates the unhappy family, *The People with the Dogs* celebrates the happy family, disproving Tolstoy's maxim that all happy families are similar, while questioning any easy distinctions between the two states. Edward's friend Walt intuitively understands the contradictions of Whitehouse, seeing it as 'the perfect still life' of 'abundant multiple life' (p. 94). There is a point where growth turns to decay, where nourishing love becomes suffocating and

where communal sharing leads to cruel exclusions.
Whitehouse has reached that point.

There the family live in the past, retelling the same old
stories for the hundredth time, with 'do you remember?'
their only refrain. Victor-Alexander has walled himself in
behind the high walls of his house named 'Solitude'. Old
Mary's children, the family outcasts, are not invited to the
wedding of two young people who have grown up together
on the estate. Oneida lives out her frenzied frustrations
through vicarious identification with the rompings of her
dogs. And Edward comes to see the great wild hops vine
that lives on every living plant and covers every building
on the property as a symbol of the ineradicable, suffocating
hold the family has over his will. A remarkable two page
description of the life of this vine concludes that

> it was a dark communication of sinew forming the body
> of a great being. It held, embraced, but did not crush
> the ground, the house, and all there brought by dogs
> and men: bones, sheathed copper wire needed for
> watering the cows, old leather shoes hidden by a
> predecessor of the Abbot, a sadiron, and all the things
> lost by this fertile careless family, and all the things
> loved by this productive, abundant family for seventy
> years; the deep ineradicable cables plunging into the hill
> soil and sending up at great distances their wires and
> threads; and the whole family and house and barns and
> the home-acres, in the great throttling of the twining
> vine. (p. 151)

Though each character takes turns hacking at this vine, it
is impossible to uproot or destroy the system without
tearing the estate apart. The vine lives parasitically but it
also holds things together – like a family, like a nation, like
a novel.

No one can deny the many ties that link one human

being to another. Nonetheless, one must also create an independent sense of self. Paradoxically, perhaps, Stead sees this creation of an independent self taking place most naturally through marriage. Where her earlier novels focused on women's need for the emotional and financial security of marriage, this book focuses on man's emotional need, a subject touched on in her portrait of Quick in *For Love Alone* but not fully elaborated until now. Like Quick, Edward roams the city streets at night, an intensely sociable being who feels himself incomplete without a companion. Robbie Grant, with his hypocritical refrain, 'All I want is a woman', is a gross caricature of the genuine but inarticulate need of these two men. For Robbie, any woman will do and so none will really do; they are as interchangeable to him as the banknotes with which he buys them. Quick and Edward, on the other hand, are unconsciously searching for a kind of 'twin soul' – a Platonic counterpart to complete their own selfhood.

In Lydia, Edward finds himself, even mistaking her eyes for his own in the car mirror after their wedding (pp. 339–340). He is surprised by the happiness she makes him feel. He tells the Solways, 'I've lived for us all. But I'd like to live for myself' (p. 332). Lydia enables him to do that. Before meeting her, he felt he had nothing to live for but in Nell's words had 'the sense just to live' (p. 306). Nell had always lived for her brother Philip. When he dies, trying to save the life of his dog Lady, Nell wants to die too and is only brought back to life through Edward's care. The tyranny of the love of brother and sister, so sadly imaged in the tragedy of Nell and Phil, provides an oblique commentary on Oneida's possessive love for her younger brother Edward. After Phil's death, Edward helps Nell learn to live for herself instead of for her brother and in the process unconsciously learns that he must leave Oneida and make a life for himself in the same way.

Similarly, Victor-Alexander, Oneida's rejected lover who

has remained on the estate in suspension since her wedding, at last takes action, writing the family that he has been 'the Prisoner of Whitehouse' (p. 342), frozen into immobility by his search for perfection within its grounds. His tearing down of Solitude's high walls signals the regeneration of Whitehouse. Its values can only survive through change. By trying to keep Whitehouse exactly as it was the family contributes to its decay. The pipes must be replaced or there is no water for the cows; buildings must be repaired or they become uninhabitable; weeds must be uprooted or they take over everywhere. Change will come whether it is welcomed or feared. When the ancient dog, Madame X, dies at last, Oneida laments, 'I lived for dogs and dogs can die!' (p. 319). Yet Lou buys her another puppy, because their lives make her as intensely happy as their deaths make her miserable. These attachments to others are what make us human: fallible, silly, but also strong.

Edward's tearful friend Dr Sam can learn from such a family. His love for Vera is not strong enough to accept her as she is, an ambitious professional singer, and so he loses her. In the bohemian circles in which the Massines move, his inability to accept her career as part of her identity is barbaric. Al Burrows laughs: 'Why should a girl with her name in lights cook eggs for an eye-doctor? He's maritally illiterate. He's a male chauvinist' (p. 56). In Robert Grant's world, Dr Sam's demands conform to the only possible plot for a true romance, but in the Massine's sphere, there are other possibilities. When Sam complains, 'She prefers success and applause to love!', Edward answers sensibly, 'Why can't you let her have all three?' (p. 230). Edward acts on these principles himself, quietly arranging his life to accommodate Lydia's work, without considering his behaviour at all unusual. The Massines are communally literate: generous, gregarious, accepting the idiosyncracies of others because they have so many themselves, intolerant only of those who fear or hate dogs. Their lives are ordered around a philosophy of abundance for all, an easy generosity because they have never gone wanting themselves.

Edward's friend Walt contends that the conditions at Whitehouse make him an exceptionally good man, whether his 'heart is big or small' (p. 94); yet these conditions have also meant that this goodness has found very little scope in which to exercise itself. Edward spends his life doing small favours for friends and family. His relatives expend far more love on their dogs than on other human beings – a state that comes to seem more pathological than funny as the novel proceeds. Often the family's love for its own seems fed by excluding others. When the pack of dogs terrorises the milkman and grocery delivery boy, the family joins in the attack rather than chastise their errant dogs. This obsessive 'love' for dogs can distort their perception of values. Oneida is bitter when she learns she cannot afford to buy a 'cure for old age' for her ancient dog. Stead writes that the family 'had always been in favour of socialised medicine but moved into an active family propaganda for it now. How angry Oneida was that the dogs of the rich could have this treatment, perhaps, and her poor dogs not. "And then there are poor old men and women," said Oneida' (p. 256). These grotesque reversals of our normal expectations are funny, and treated gently here. Even seemingly disinterested activity, Stead seems to be suggesting, may often be motivated by obscurely selfish needs.

Certainly the family's inherited money insulates them from the rat race of *A Little Tea, a Little Chat*, whose characters love the United States, 'intensely, ferociously, with terror and greed'.[5] The Massines love their country intimately, with a gaiety that comes from security and knowledge, because it is their home. But their experience leads them to make the same mistake made by Robbie Grant and his associates – to assume that the rest of the world thinks and lives as they do. Edward's own comfort causes him to conclude that 'Communism is a great mistake; when one fellow has the property, he's ever so much better off' (p. 25). This on the very day a man has murdered his wife on Edward's street because they had no place to live, while Edward owns three houses! Stead shows the limitations of Edward's good nature by exposing ironies like this and contrasting the abundance of his family's existence with the scarcities of life in the slums and the bathhouses of New York. Edward himself is disturbed by his encounter with a man freezing in a doorway on a night when he would have taken a shelterless dog or cat home with him. But he feels powerless to do anything on his own. And the communal dream of Whitehouse is clearly a privileged retreat that relies for its continuation on a selective hospitality.

The People with the Dogs is very much a postwar novel, about picking up the pieces of civilian life after years of unnatural, hyped-up aggression against a clearly defined enemy; about deciding what to do with your life now you have a life of your own again; about the tremendous pressures on the housing and job markets exerted by returned soldiers; about the crisis of the Left in a period when people are sick of controversy and think that a 'return to normalcy' is the best they can look forward to. When Edward stumbles on the May Day parade, he feels the discouragement born of knowing that they 'now had to begin all from the beginning' (p. 107). With his friend Philip Christy, an old radical turned disappointed drunk, Edward makes a tour of Philip's old circle, some still true to their beliefs, others having fallen away, but all alike discouraged, defeated, having retreated from public activity into private despair. He visits the puppet maker, Waldemar Block, 'a terribly hungry man' (p. 222), who can never get enough to eat. Against his wife's will, Waldemar talks of his experiences during the war as a candidate for the Reichstag who had fled the Nazi regime, escaping across the border to safety, followed by a move to the United States and life as an apolitical toymaker. His terrible hunger seems a compelling image of the emptiness experienced by almost all the characters in *The People with the Dogs*. He disciplines it by eating well only on certain special days; they cannot afford to satisfy it.

Paradoxically, the price of his freedom in the United States is the quelling of his need to speak out on political issues and the transforming of that hunger to act into a hunger to consume. He becomes a potent symbol of the change from prewar social movements to postwar passivity. His speech has been stopped; but his hunger cannot be appeased by bread alone.

Oneida tries to quell her hunger through lavishing affection on her dogs. Like Sam's love of children, Oneida's 'cult of dogs' disguises a potentially destructive possessive urge. No doubt Lou gives her dogs to protect himself. Although Oneida argues that love of dogs makes us more selfless, she knows at heart – and sometimes admits – that in fact through domestication 'we have ruined them, dithtorted them, thwarted them . . .' (p. 100), her lisp here providing a mirroring distortion of her own. Stead seems to endorse this view in an eerie passage recording the dogs' baying welcome to the moon as it rises over the sleepers at Whitehouse. Whatever their varied history, the narrator asserts, they are

> at all times dressed in their masters' insolence, and insolence their sole profession, a hundred court fools, hangmen and watchmen and killers; so these hundred dogs, whether chained like poor Charlie or free like Madame X, furiously, unhappily in the dark gardens, stirred by an ancient passion, fear and awe beyond their feeble souls, barked at the moon, at the furtive shadows come alive, at the strangeness of a world born again at night, in which their poor minds, seduced and debauched,

were stirred and so rankled. The wolf came back.
(p. 208)

The People with the Dogs shows that people are like their
dogs, distorted in strange ways by the civilisation they have
built for themselves, hungering for fulfilments they do not
know how to achieve. They have disciplined the 'wolf' in
themselves to compromise in various ways, becoming
sycophantic toadies, artists (official fools) or thugs. But
such transformations have not brought them the satisfactions
they sought. The rewards of 'a dog's life' are meagre
indeed. But the pessimism of such a conclusion is balanced,
even overridden, by the parallel assertion that things need
not be so. Even 'poor minds, seduced and debauched' can
give birth to a new and better world. Part of literature's
task is to stir and rankle our sleeping desires, acting like
the moon, to awaken us to other possibilities than those
realised in the world we know. *The People with the Dogs*
pokes gentle fun at the insularity and protected quality of
American life that makes the United States at once so
generous yet so intolerant. The 'puzzleheaded' girls,
innocent arrogants abroad, continue Stead's consideration
of this increasingly important American paradox.

Puzzleheaded girls

Each of the four novellas included in *The Puzzleheaded Girl*
focuses on confused young American women, unable to
reconcile parental and societal versions of the world with
their own experience. Published as a collection in 1968, the
stories move from the twenties to the sixties, covering
roughly the same period as Stead's four American novels.
But whereas the earlier novels showed us the interior lives
of Louisa, Teresa and Letty, allowing the reader to perceive
the world through their eyes, these stories allow no access

into their central characters. They are viewed entirely from the outside, through what they do and say and how they appear to others. The result is distancing. Each woman remains as much of an enigma to us as to those she puzzles within the story.

Honor Lawrence, the puzzleheaded girl of the title story, could be an American Teresa Hawkins, arriving to apply for a secretarial position carrying an art book and appealing to the sympathy of the quixotic Debrett, who hires her against his better judgement. Like Teresa, Honor appears to be hopelessly naive, the victim of a cultural deprivation so severe she has no sense at all of customary social behaviour. By taking everyone at his word, by believing the platitudes she has been taught, she shows up the artificiality of social conventions. She teaches others to see themselves in a new light. Because Honor wants a unified life, the kind of freedom America supposedly offers its citizens, the still idealistic Debrett welcomes her as a 'kind of miracle' but his partner Tom Zero, always the pragmatist, finds her ignorance irritating. He wishes she could be like everyone else, telling Debrett: 'Let her do her work and keep her morals for home'.[6] Zero's name suggests his potential from Stead's point of view; he will do anything to maintain his comfortable social dominance. Debrett, in contrast, can make money for others but never for himself.

Because she cannot make Zero's divisions between private and public, Honor is sensitive to abuses that others take so much for granted they do not even see them as abuses. This trait is particularly interesting for the reader today, at a time when contemporary feminism has alerted us to notice and so refuse to tolerate the same kinds of sexual harassment that Honor rejects. When another of her bosses, Arthur Good, 'ran his hand lightly down her hip and touched her stockinged knee' (p. 14), she ran out of the office, to his mild amusement. But when she hits a client for trying to fondle her, she is reprimanded and told to behave herself (p. 20). Neither incident carries authorial commentary. To the characters within the story, Honor's behaviour signals her odd insistence on an independence they have long ago given up for themselves, if they are women, or that they think inappropriate in a woman, if they are men. To a reader in the eighties, however, Honor's touchiness is understandable. An intrinsically corrupt society labels her integrity 'puzzleheaded', and so eventually drives her to fit that label. Recent feminist research has made us familiar with the means our society has developed for driving women, in particular, mad. Honor's first transformation from the poverty-stricken immigrant girl Rosina Tomasseo to the proud Boston-born Honor Lawrence showed the strength of her will to succeed, to transform herself to meet the requirements of the American Dream. But her later transformations from innocent schoolgirl to ghoul and diseased prostitute, in the eyes of others if not in fact, show how impossible that dream was for anyone who wished to live with honour. As Debrett's English friend puts it, 'Hard is life for those who can't eat dirt' (p. 56).

But the story is less about Honor herself than about the efforts of others to understand her. As her husband Jay says: 'We don't understand many people in a lifetime. We don't love many people in a lifetime. It's a dreadful thought. Life rushing past, populations of people and we're indifferent, blind; we might be asleep or dead. We are dead when we don't love' (p. 64). Here he expresses Stead's recurrent equation of a metaphorical blindness with the sleep of death. The writer's creativity can waken us from this blindness, making us see, just as love itself provides us with a fresh perspective on everything. Honor, her own work of art, also wakens people to that effort of understanding that for some can lead to love, to an engagement with the world around them.

The last of the many characters who attempt to interpret

Honor is Debrett's second wife Mari, whom Stead has claimed is modelled on herself as Debrett is on Blake.[7] She sees Honor as 'the ragged, wayward heart of woman that doesn't want to be caught and hasn't been caught' (p. 67), the spirit of independence that has been distorted, diseased and then killed by a society that cannot tolerate its existence because it challenges the present order of things. Debrett himself prefers a more romantic interpretation, seeing her as a kind of holy fool, a reminder of human fallibility. His first wife Beatrice, who feels herself cheated by life, sees her as 'a repressed girl who is hunted by lechers, criminals and hags', who concentrates in herself 'all the horror and misery which is life itself' (p. 52). Honor's brother sees her as a strange kind of saint and her husband Jay Hewett as a 'work of art' (p. 63) that he was born to understand. To Jay, she was sui generis, a self-created miracle. In his interpretation, Honor, lacking the self-centredness to create artefacts apart from herself, turned all her great creativity into making her life a work of art. This theory, too, fits well with current ideas about the diverting of female creativity away from the channels approved for the male into channels designed to continue their own objectification as playthings for men. Honor's brother wins a prize for his paintings; Honor must be content with the creation of a self intriguing to men.

The effect of all these different responses to 'the puzzleheaded girl' is to create a composite picture, not so much of a single individual, as of a symbolic one. Debrett thinks he sees her everywhere, even after reports of her sordid death in a winter doorway. While each character interprets Honor Lawrence in relation to his or her own personal need, the reader can fit the pieces together to form a more comprehensive pattern. Although her gender is clearly the chief determinant of her fate, it is not the only one. She is the child of 'crazed poverty' (p. 36), of a tyrannical father who begrudged his children food, whose miserliness drove his wife to suicide and his children to flee – all save the youngest, fourteen-year-old Honor. He keeps her locked up when she is not out at work to repay him the money she has cost him in room and board over the years of her childhood. Her poverty makes her vulnerable to the advances of men and women who offer to keep her, and prevents her from finding a better job to keep herself. Yet paradoxically, it seems also to have made her 'austere, pure and high-minded. She believes in what she says' (p. 37). Not knowing what it means to buy something for herself in a shop, not knowing that such things as happy families or rich families exist, she feels no temptation to sell out and cannot understand compromise in others. Her integrity functions to reproach the complacencies of others, who respond according to the fineness of their own natures. Zero and his wife, thoroughly conformist, protect themselves from such deviancy by calling Honor an extravagant tramp, but Beatrice and Debrett, envying her her freedom from the Zero's world, feel spurred themselves to try to escape.

Eventually, however, Honor learns that her vision of life was false, that the people continually telling her to be 'sensible', far from being fools, in fact knew much more about how the world actually worked than she did. Herself rejected by the man she loved after she had borne his baby, she rejected love itself as 'all lies' (p. 66) and disappeared to die in the street. Whereas Teresa's quest found fulfilment, Honor's ends in personal defeat. Yet Debrett cannot believe in her death and her story continues to haunt him.

Parallel to her story of hungry wandering, lies the story of Debrett's unhappy first marriage with Beatrice. Beatrice, middle-class, married to a kind man, secure, would seem to have everything Honor lacks, yet she too is miserable, suffering from post-partum depression after the birth of her first child and feeling suffocated by her family. Debrett is jealous of the child. She is exhausted by its demands and gets little help from him. She cannot shut her eyes to 'the boredom and unfairness' (p. 51) of marriage; but neither can she rouse herself to seek what she truly wants. Debrett agrees that 'it sounds a pretty miserable world for women' (p. 51) but no one can help another to freedom. Both Honor and Beatrice find themselves trapped in uncongenial roles, beat against their cages, but cannot find their way out of the double binds society has constructed for them. Conformity and rebellion alike prove dead ends.

If 'The Puzzleheaded Girl' sees no way out of suffering, the conventional happy ending of 'The Dianas' seems even bleaker. At first Lydia, a giddy, thirty-year-old virgin half-heartedly in search of a husband, finds herself trapped in the role of girlish flirt that she has learned from her mother. Only her maiden aunt's death calms her mounting hysteria, providing her with a more sober ideal on which to model herself. With her mother, she had always laughed at the insufficiencies of the men who approached them. The circumstances of her aunt's death make her think that perhaps they have laughed too much and too unthinkingly. Lydia says she wants 'a man to look up to and who will teach me' (p. 76) – a kind of father figure – and eventually finds a man willing to take complete responsibility for her. The story concludes: 'Presently it was as if her old life had never been; and she had grown up in his house; and it was many years before she thought about their union or found anything in it extraordinary' (p. 112). The price she pays for this calm is an absolute rejection of her mother, her friends and her past. With her marriage she assumes an entirely new identity, created for her by her husband just as her past self appeared to have been created for her by her mother. Lydia has acted incapable of making up her mind, flighty and superficial, because her mother's experience had taught them that men preferred such behaviour. By its means the mother had won Lydia's father. But such methods fail Lydia. She finds her man through utter passivity.

For Lydia the only escape from her domineering mother comes through the acquisition of a domineering husband. While it is a relief to see the nervous Lydia find some calm at last, it is disturbing to see that calm bought at the price of her selfhood. Throughout her story, Lydia's behaviour contradicts her stated aim. She enjoys the company of her women friends, preferring them to the men, whom she teases, ignores and tortures, but to whom she is basically indifferent. Yet society dictates that women are her rivals and man her goal, so against all the experience of her 31 years, she submits her life to upholding a truism she knows in her heart to be false.

Linda, of 'The Girl From the Beach', returns like Lydia from fruitless searching on the Continent to a safe marriage at home. But Linda's story is complicated by its interweaving with the persecutions of the McCarthy era, in which friends 'gave names' to save themselves. Linda's personal history contains similar betrayals. As a nine-year-old girl, she was raped by a friend of her parents at their place on the beach. The rape results from Linda's stealing of Laura Deans' red slippers. In the little girl's imagination these slippers represent all the glamour and beauty of the cosmopolitan world. When she calls in the father of a friend to show him the slippers, he rapes her. Gilbert and Gubar trace the motif of the red shoes in women's writing back to Snow White, where the Queen dances to her death in fiery red shoes. Handed down from one generation of women to another, the shoes represent female rebellion, the taking of an active role forbidden women, the making of art; but they also represent the punishment for that rebellion – death. As Margaret Atwood's *Lady Oracle* puts it: 'The real red shoes, the feet punished for dancing. You could dance, or you could have the love of a good man'.[8] If you danced, you had your feet cut off; if you married, the curtailment of your freedom took a subtler form. Linda learns the lesson of these crippling alternatives early. The punishment for taking the red shoes (of initiative, of dreaming of a wider sphere of activity, of seizing beauty for oneself) is rape – humiliation, fear and silence. Linda comments: 'I didn't know I couldn't have a baby. I waited for two or three years, expecting to have a baby. I was so frightened I would begin to swell like the women, and my mother would scold me' (p. 254). The combination of an adult awareness of the tyranny of biology with the child's fear of a scolding is heartbreaking.

Linda and Lydia do their best to dance a little in Europe before returning to the death-in-life of marriage to a good man back home. But their dancing has already been inhibited by their infantilisation. Taking to heart her mother's advice to be a 'vegetable', Linda remains as ignorant of her surroundings in Paris as she is of politics. The fate Letty Fox saw claiming her friends and feared for herself has come to pass for Linda's generation. Linda has fled an arranged American marriage to seek something more in Europe, but cannot break out of the American community there. As Martin Dean describes her: 'She has no more sense of direction than a packet of firecrackers, firing off in all directions' (p. 239). In this she seems typical of her generation, 'crazy American bohemian kids' (p. 226) bumming their way through Europe in the belief that the world owes them a living because their country 'saved the world' by winning World War II.

The Beach had been a community of leftists committed to social change to improve the lot of the people. But as Linda's rape proves, the communal solidarity that the Deans remember with nostalgia did not necessarily extend to women or children. Despite such failures to realise this ideal, the dream itself remains good, yet even that is no longer tolerated in McCarthy's America. Linda describes the lynch riots, the pressure to be 'upwardly mobile', the charge of 'un-Americanism' with a naiveté that shows she herself can never have been a part of those discussions at the Beach. The traditions have not been passed on through her. Instead, she naively repeats American propaganda: 'there aren't any poor in America' and 'we have to help everyone' (p. 222). Laura's probing questions expose the hollowness of this philosophy but Linda cannot conceive of a perspective beyond America's.

In this trait she complements Barby, the other 'girl from the beach' who figures largely in this story. Linda's cultivated babyishness is the flip side of Barby's streetwise knowingness. Linda's Eastern beach, of leftish intellectuals, complements Barby's Californian beach, where at 16 she was living with a community of writers, who made big money writing smut and sensation stories. Barby, George Paul's fourth wife, and Linda, the girl he next wants to marry, go off together, stealing George's car. Barby, the professional adventuress, and Linda, the professional victim, both land on their feet, but for all their frenzied searching each remains essentially a 'puzzleheaded girl', unhappy with her lot yet unable to change it. Although much like men, as Letty says, they are compelled to act differently to meet men's expectations. Whether a man prefers girls, like George Paul, or women, like Martin Dean, the idea that the opposite sex must be different remains a constant that confuses their relations.

Like Lydia, Linda eventually takes refuge in amnesia. After her return to America, she sees Paris as a 'waking dream' (p. 284), the events of which she can barely remember. The dream inspired by the red slippers cannot be made a reality in the world Stead describes. And so Linda rewrites her past to conform to conventional expectations in the last words of the story.

Unlike the other three stories, 'The Right-Angled Creek' never presents its 'puzzleheaded girl' directly, yet Hilda Dilley haunts this story's characters even more dramatically through her absence than the others do through their presences. As the subtitle indicates, this is a 'sort of ghost story'. Hilda Dilley has been driven mad by an unhappy marriage, a disease contracted from her husband, a dead baby, her husband's desertion. Imagining herself Pocahantas, the Indian princess, she tries to murder her parents, but instead of winning freedom through this rebellion, she finds herself incarcerated in the local asylum. A neighbour explains her madness: 'She thought people were her enemies' (p. 160). Thereafter her unhappy spirit seems to haunt the place, determined to drive out any human intruders who try to settle there.

But the narrative leaves it in doubt whether Hilda is the initiator of the place's curse or only another of its victims. The story falls into two halves, the first treating the Davies family's summer in the cottage, with Sam Parsons as a guest and the second, the following summer when Sam and his wife Clare are renting the place. Although the Davies find the place 'a green paradise' (p. 134) and an asylum, they bring their troubles with them, so that their tragedy hardly requires a supernatural explanation. Laban, an alcoholic, deserts his family for a binge and their dream falls to pieces once more. Yet his wife Ruth, not an imaginative type, feels an uncanny presence in the house, which she visualises as a 'huge hairy man in the attic' (p. 143). The mysteries accumulate during the Parsons' tenure: knives hidden everywhere, strange footfalls at night, an increasingly powerful humming as of a strange insect during the day, a mysterious force trying to push Clare downstairs, a wolf called up from nowhere, a death by poison ivy, a broken arm. The Parsons' greater attachment to the place seems to call up a greater resistence from it.

The story's first half describes what drives the Labans into the country – their 'friends'' enjoyment of Laban's degradation: 'it's inhuman joy to them to take him away

from us and to kill him with drink' (p. 143); while the
second suggests some of what may have driven them out of
it – the knowledge that nature too 'breeds horrors' (p. 147).
This untended farm is a refuge for all the wildlife driven
from the cultivated farms in the neighbourhood. Everything
wild, untamed, finds sanctuary here. The little locked
room holding Hilda's belongings seems to be 'the smiling
heart of that ineffable house' (p. 152), a place where the
unconscious desires of the underwater world seek the
surface and occasionally flood. Yet Clare thinks too that if
the devil really is the Lord of the Flies, they must be very
close to his hole in that place, close to the genesis of evil as
well as teeming but unconscious life. To Clare, premonitions
are merely an 'unrecognised part of nature . . . . Few
heard them; they were there' (p. 149). Yet even she, so
open to nature and so tolerant of life in all its manifestations,
cannot bear the heightened hearing conferred by this
enchanted place in the woods. Society, for all its faults,
remains the true refuge for human beings, here as in all
Stead's writing.

Each of these stories, then, examines a myth of escape
from social constrictions, only to reject it as unsatisfactory.
Neither escape into a bohemian expatriate life, roaming
around Europe, nor escape into marriage with a man who
will shoulder all responsibility, nor escape from the city
into the country can be a true escape, for people continue
to carry their problems with them wherever they go.

Yet these stories also reveal the inadequacy of reducing
everything to the personal level alone. Although Lydia and
Linda and even Honor eventually believe that there must
be something the matter with them that prevents them
from finding what other people seem to have, their stories
suggest that their problems derive from their times. They
have been convinced that they are the problem and that
they must adjust to the world as they find it. When the
disparity between what they are told and what they know

confuses them, they are called 'puzzleheaded', as if the problem lay in them and not in the disparity that first confused them. Victims of the Cold War, they live in a time of official silence on all the great issues that concern them, a silence so enveloping they have become persuaded that politics is not a matter of their daily lives, but merely something external to them in which they have no interest. Privatised and infantilised, these girls turn their frustrations inward, destroying themselves, or turn them outward against an individual man or a parent. But the stories continue to display the contradictions that official orthodoxies seek to explain away. They provide the missing sense of context that these characters lack. Through refusing to focus any story on a single figure, Stead avoids the trap of making individuality the chief issue here. Instead, she balances numerous characters against one another, demonstrating the intricate webs of interrelationships weaving even the most apparently solitary of figures – such as Honor Lawrence – into the social fabric.

7 In the Hall of Mirrors

After a long middle period, inspired by her lucky meeting with Blake, in which she considered the multiple dimensions of love in our century, Stead's return to Europe after the war brought about a return to the Depression-inspired themes of her earliest fiction. Coming from the relative ease of wartime America, Stead was shocked by the poverty and hunger of postwar Europe. This shock seems to have stimulated a reconsideration of hunger as a drive even more powerful than love. Parallel to this shift from satisfaction to deprivation, emerges a shift in her portrayal of women. Unlike the sturdily iconoclastic heroines of her middle period, the women of this final period outwardly at least conform more closely to male stereotypes of female behaviour. Nellie Cotter is a 'bleeding heart', a 'sobsister', a lesbian and a 'castrating bitch' yet finally cannot be confined by any of these labels. Lilia Trollope is a victim, but a victim who eventually finds the strength to take her freedom. Eleanor Herbert is a 'suburban wife', but her desperate adherence to convention only serves to show its inadequacies.

Stead portrays all these characters as trapped in a hall of mirrors, returning to the symbol for entrapment she had used in her first novel, *Seven Poor Men of Sydney*. These characters hardly recognise themselves in the distorted images that their world reflects back to them, yet adjusting to the mirror seems easier than shattering it for the reflections it provides remain their only confirmation of their existence in society's eyes. To turn away from the mirror is to risk annihilation. It is no accident that Sheila Rowbotham uses the same metaphor in *Woman's Consciousness, Man's World*, to argue that 'The prevailing social order stands as a great and resplendent hall of mirrors. It owns and occupies the world as it is and the world as it is seen and heard . . . . In order to create an alternative an oppressed group must at once shatter the self-reflecting world which encircles it and, at the same time, project its own image onto history.'[1] Stead's novels show how difficult this process is. Everywhere her characters turn they encounter further distorting reflections. They are alone because as women they have been taught not to trust one another. They are powerless to act because they fear they will lose their femininity if they smash things, or if they do smash the mirror of femininity, like Nellie Cotter, they find themselves automatically reflected in another mirror as witch. Yet although Stead's characters remain trapped in their hall of mirrors, her readers may feel themselves freed, because in Stead's novels they can see the hall of mirrors described for what it is – a conjuror's trick. And when the trick is exposed, the illusion vanishes.

Cotters' England: Humbug and humblepie

'Cotters' England' – 'the England of the depressed that starved you all to wraiths'[2] – gives twisted life to Stead's last great novel. Thoroughly steeped in English idioms, the English landscape and English politics, the book repositions some of Stead's most compelling themes in what is for her a new setting. Where Stead's last four American books had plumbed the depths of the 'moral bottom' on which American hopes for change were grounded during the Cold War years, *Cotters' England* shows the same period refracted through English eyes. In the Afterword to the Australian paperback edition, Terry Sturm argues convincingly that the novel's subtitle might well have been 'Why England hasn't had a revolution'.[3] As usual in Stead, the novel turns about the lives of individual people, so compellingly drawn that they seem to exist independently from their author, yet so placed against one another that their lives take on a significance for us that they never can for them.

Nellie Cook, née Cotter – Stead's most horrifying creation – dominates the novel with her endless, spellbinding and malevolent talk. Less vicious than Robbie Grant, she is far more terrible, both more compelling and better-intentioned. Like Sam Pollit, she is a well-meaning egotist blind to the damage she wreaks. But unlike Sam, she has an adult's mind. She lacks his fatal innocence. Where Sam is a child of the daylight world, Nellie lives for the night. The last of Stead's marathon talkers, Nellie is also the most complex. Although wrong, she is hard to refute. Although hideous, she remains attractive. Although wicked, she retains our pity.

As in all Stead's books a story unfolds itself tangentially, through apparently random conversations and confrontations, building to moments of crisis and falling away again, creating the rhythms appropriate to itself. Nellie consumes herself and others with her frenetic energy, her gargantuan appetite for life, with her fears of being abandoned by her husband, George Cook, a prominent Labour leader, and of losing her job as a journalist on a radical paper. She uses up people the way she smokes cigarettes, sucking them dry and then throwing them away.

Near the end of the book it appears she might break out of the self-destructive routine her life has become. George sends for her to join him in Geneva where he has taken a new job, resolutely leaving Cotters' England behind him. In typical Stead fashion we learn the end through hearsay long after the events are over when Mrs McMahon, the cleaning lady who is pining away with her hopeless love for the absent George, asks one of the women she cleans for if she has heard from him. It turns out that Nellie did lose her husband, but not in the way she had feared. He died accidentally in a ski accident overseas. The papers did not print the picture of Nellie and her brother Tom, smiling for the camera, hand in hand at the funeral. Nellie returned to England, lost interest in politics and with the encouragement of her window cleaner became 'interested in the problems of the unknowable' (p. 352). She remains trapped in her hall of mirrors, Cotters' England, where even 'the unknowable' only reflects back herself.

Cotters' England is one of Stead's most tightly written books because the story it tells is one of entrapment. None of its characters can break free from their class or from the outlook it has given them. The devastating irony in the middle-class housewives' discussion of their cleaning lady's interest in George Cook says it all: 'one said, I think she was in love with George Cook; but they could not accept this idea; a servant in love with George Cook who had been described in the foreign press, when he died, as a "great fighter for the British working class, who turned many to socialism by his ready forceful expositions"' (pp. 351–52). George's fight to wrest 'their England' from 'them' for the people of 'Cotters' England' was never fully understood, even by his friends, even by his wife. Not even he, perhaps, understood fully what the implications of the struggle might be. Undisturbed by his death, Nellie's life goes on much as before. The window cleaner has been there from the novel's first page, receiving Nellie's cast-off gifts and her interest. Nellie's line has always been a pretence of exploring the unknowable, and Nellie's bond with Tom the unbreakable one. A Stead novel does not live for its conclusion, but for its everyday life as enacted on the page. In *Cotters' England*, it is precisely the conduct of that everyday life, the force of habit, that defeats George's vision of change.

'Cotters' England' finds its most dramatic embodiment in Nellie and in Tom, her reflection or 'shadow self' (p. 256). But it lives as well through all the varied characters who form their circle – through their immediate family, their lovers and their friends. The novel's dominant image is the hall of mirrors. None of the characters' relationships seems able to escape it. Tom and Nellie mirror one another in the destructive bonds they form with others, Tom in his passivity mirroring his mother and Nellie in her aggressiveness mirroring her father and their sister Peggy in her calculating craziness mirroring both. Nellie marries a man whom others see as the image of her father, and she repeats her mother's patterns of behaviour with him as he repeats her father's with her. Nellie and George live in a household with his first wife Eliza posing as his sister just as Tom and his mistress Marion live with her husband Constantine, Tom posing as Marion's brother. After Marion's death, the three men who loved her all choose to marry at the same time. And in the most devastating scene of all, Caroline's suicide mirrors the death of the Indian boy from Jago's bohemian circle and of the girl who died for Johnny, Nellie's lesbian lover and rival.

In one of the novel's central scenes the 'fatal brother and sister' chance upon a country fair and entering the Palace of Mirrors confront themselves. The strangely distorted outer forms seem such accurate reflections of inner truth that Nellie exclaims: 'Why, thank God, Tom, it is not the Hall of Truth' (p. 189). Tom appears as a 'playing-card King', Nellie as a 'spindling hatchet witch' and 'black raven', images that accompany them throughout the novel. Nellie is displeased: 'They're distortions of human beings! Why do we like it, Tom?' (p. 190) – and her question reverberates throughout the novel. Why do people put up with such cramping lives, such distorting poverty, such unappeased hunger? Can they really find themselves in the images their society offers them?

During an argument with Nellie, George phrases the same question in terms of Stead's recurrent metaphor of frustrated appetite, asking angrily: 'Why doesn't my country offer me a square meal?' (p. 215). The grotesque chicken dinner shared by Tom and his family in the Bridgehead home where they grew up answers George's question while vividly imaging the deprivation of which he speaks. No one knows how to cook it. Tom can never remember eating one at home. In their ignorance, they ruin its flavour, boiling away its nourishment without fully cooking it and finally eat a miserable, half-cold, saltless and incomplete meal, for the old mother in her senility has thrown out the cooked potatoes in order to wash the serving dish. She prefers a tidy house to the mess that food entails. No wonder her husband was always 'a hungry man'. Very late in the story, it is revealed that she starved her children to buy the pretentious furniture that crowds her rented house and that her favourite pastime with her children was denying that she loved them, while greedily trying to live through their experiences, for she herself never ventured beyond the block, being an 'old-fashioned woman' and proud of her servitude. Here are the same traits praised in the English working class by Stewart in *House of All Nations*: a misunderstanding of their role so pervasive they can feel proud of their chains.

George's first wife, Eliza, seems to be speaking for Stead when she speculates: 'I've always had the thought . . . that hunger is a greater passion than love; and I've been surprised not to hear them talk about the distortions produced by hunger, the sublimations and disguised forms of hunger. It's a primitive need, you can live without all but food . . . . So it must take very diverse forms in us, especially in a childhood and youth of semi-starvation' (p. 211). *Cotters' England* describes these diverse forms, questioning Nellie's glib cliché that 'man does not live by bread alone'. One of George's first political acts was to introduce tomatoes and lettuce into the diets of his resisting fellow workers. After visiting the Continent, he wants to buy cook books, to study the art his people have so much neglected. Nellie, who lives on tea, cigarettes and gin, resists these foreign importations as sturdily as she does his Marxist theory. For all her insistence on a grounding in material reality, she remains more out of touch with it than he. As George suggests, she seems more taken with the bohemian pose of rebellion than with a genuine urge to change the world she has inherited.

As a young girl hungering for more than either her family or her northern coal town, Bridgehead, could offer her, she had fed indiscriminately on whatever seemed to offer a way out, trying the Fascist party before converting to Jago's libertarian anarchism. Stead comments: 'Hunger will prey on garbage, rather than be extinguished in death. But Nellie had not called it garbage, she called it knowledge' (p. 294). Again and again Stead returns to this theme of misnaming and misreading reality. Nellie, who prides herself on her insight, is the worst offender. Her youthful diet of self-indulgent sentimentalism has spoiled her appetite for more wholesome fare. Her thinking remains a tangle of Jago's maxims – Introspect!, Experience! – and the common-sense clichés of English pragmatism. These lead her to a kind of emotional cannibalism. Rather than starve, she feeds on others' weaknesses. Tom describes her as a vampire, who after devouring his heart is now 'scurrying around from one body to another, hungry and thirsty, and you'll do anything to still the pain' (p. 248).

Genuinely committed to the cause of her own class, Nellie gradually emerges as its own worst enemy. She is a 'sobsister' (pp. 214 and 237), distracted from working for structural change by the details of individual suffering she sees around her. By focusing on effects rather than causes, she remains within the very territory staked out for her by the hated enemy, the bourgeoisie. Pride makes her reject charity, patriotism makes her reject criticism, sentimentality makes her reject theory. She is left with nothing but herself. And only in nightmares does she suspect the truth about that, dreaming of descending a staircase into the darkness ahead of her (p. 345).

Nellie poisons all around her, undermining the cause of her class from within, because she can only see class conflict in personal terms: herself as a martyr, 'maimed and glad of it' (p. 295), a heroine on a stage above the rabble. Accepting external definitions of her class as illiterate, more feeling than thinking, she rejects analysis as bourgeois. She mistakes all the traits resulting from her class's oppression – all the distortions of their humanity into narrow and ignorant paths – for characteristics intrinsic to her class itself and therefore rejects any efforts to improve their collective lot as a selling out to middle-class values.

She takes a similar stand on women's issues. She welcomes the prostitute Venna as her true sister, vicariously enjoying her degradation; but does her best to undermine the efforts of Caroline and Camilla to work for concrete change. Stead shows that Nellie's radicalism is as far as it is possible to go from genuine radicalism. By mouthing clichés she undermines substantial action. Her type give the women's movement and the Left a bad name. Similarily, Nellie's lesbianism is as far as it is possible to go from true sisterhood: she 'loves' women only to destroy them. This is the meaning of the horrifying scene that drives Caroline to her death. The circling of naked women in the moonlight is a travesty of the true female friendship that Caroline seeks. Significantly Eliza, who offers such friendship, has been excluded from these revels, while the vicious Johnny, who frightens even Nellie, is one of the ringleaders.

Nellie as cackling witch, self-dramatising poisoner and haunting bird of prey hounds the innocent Caroline to her death in order to prove her power to Johnny but Caroline's suicide note resists Nellie's vision of the world even as it grants her the death she desired. Caroline upholds her own vision of honour against Nellie's denial, though she knows 'I can say nothing to you, for you are inside your cell of glass' (p. 304). Trapped in her hall of mirrors, Nellie sees everywhere only her own reflection – that of a being starved and twisted into the most horrible deformation. In *The People with the Dogs*, Stead makes fun of the simplistic idea that criminals cannot be held responsible for their actions because their society has somehow forced them into lawlessness by denying them the development of their full human potential. In fact, this is the kind of argument Nellie favours, only she takes it one step further to insist that only those corrupted by their financial need are worthy of our respect. The others must be hypocrites or overprotected from Nellie's 'reality', which is one of unmitigated horror. *Cotters' England* exposes this thinking for the dangerous nonsense it is. But Stead does believe that we can only understand individuals through analysing the forces that have shaped them. And that once we understand, it may be harder to judge. Poverty does not warp everyone. Eliza came through equal deprivation apparently unscathed, yet precisely because she does know what Nellie's struggle has been, Eliza can love her while deploring her descent into darkness. Again her stance seems similar to Stead's.

Nellie's wrong-headedness at first amuses, then annoys and finally horrifies the reader, just as it does her brother Tom, before leading us to pity her as the victim of her illusions. Nellie does not belong with the people she presumes to speak for. She stands out like 'a draggled peacock in a serious busy barnyard' (p. 269) and attracts derision. Yet the novel also warns us against taking her type too lightly. Tom cannot believe she might do real harm. She proves him wrong.

Laughing away her many betrayals of him, Tom teases her: 'Whenever I see them asking how it is that people confess in political trials, I laugh and think: Whoever caught Nellie, she'd confess. She'd confess so much they'd have to stuff their ears, shut up shop, they'd hear such a damnable Arabian Nights, they'd go out of – they'd go out and get drunk' (pp. 81–82). This is both funny and frightening. In the Cold War context in which this story takes place, where Camilla suspects that the window cleaner's apparently innocent questions may be those of a spy, Nellie's 'mania for confession' reflects that of her times. As she says, 'the muck-raking and social-worker epoch is ended' (p. 259). This is the age of 'Introspection', of blaming yourself if you're unhappy, of 'Confessing' to purge your soul, of 'Submission' to your fate – Nellie's three magic words for poisoning her victims. More recently, Christopher Lasch has called it the age of Narcissism. Like Narcissus, Tom and Nellie find themselves trapped by their reflected images in the mirrors of themselves. The counterpart of all this inward-looking is the scapegoating of those who do still believe in change. Here too Nellie leads the attack, charging that 'Marxism is cruel, because it doesn't care about the individual' (p. 295), the theory can't 'explain the unknowable' (p. 235) and anyway 'political action is wrong' (p. 157).

Cotters' England is Stead's most ironical book. The reader soon learns to believe the opposite of whatever Nellie says. When she attacks a Labour leader, her editor or another journalist for being a fool or a loser, we hear from independent commentary later that these are exceptionally astute or successful people. After she brags of her ideal marriage, we watch an uneasy union disintegrate before our eyes. When she speaks of love and friendship we learn to beware. Her attacks on others expose her own sins. Obsessed with unburdening others of their illusions so that they might see her version of 'truth', Nellie is Stead's most self-deceived character. Trapped in her own illusions, with the roof of her house collapsing in upon her and nowhere else to go, Nellie presents a bleak image of postwar England. She and her brother alike croon destructive songs of love and death to steal the hearts and dull the initiative of their listeners. Their own hopes for Cythera shipwrecked, their siren songs now bring disaster to all who listen. Eliza's analysis of the struggles of her youth still holds true for the England of her maturity: 'We just couldn't get along on humblepie and humbug, but that's all we knew' (p. 212).

Through her ironic portrait of Nellie, Stead destroys the new versions of 'humblepie and humbug' that enable the old status quo to maintain its dominance while she poses the real questions that faced England in 1966 and today through George. He tells Nellie: 'You're helping your lords and masters by talking a lot of frill about patriotism. Whose country is it? Whose pound sterling is it? Whose empire is it? Whose revenues are they?' (p. 216). These are the questions that could lead the way out of the hall of distorting mirrors. But no one in Cotters' England can turn away from the mirrors, fearing that for them as for the Lady of Shalott, the alternative to illusion may be death. Tom's final 'horrifying tale' expresses this fear. When the harmless old man who imagined he owned houses is finally convinced by an interfering busybody that in fact he owns no houses, he tries to drown himself in despair. Yet *Cotters' England* as a whole shows us that it is far more frightening to stay locked in a hall of mirrors where it is 'bad manners to talk about the bomb' (p. 72), than to shatter the mirrors, risk flying glass but get out in the open and see where you are.

Stead's working title for *Cotters' England* was 'Uncle Syme'. In the published version, Uncle Simon's story appears to be a minor subplot, subordinated to Nellie's, yet complementing it and powerful in its own right. This decent, hard-working man has supported his sister's family, paying their rent and contributing his salary to their upkeep for 40 years. When his sister dies, his niece Peggy steals his remaining savings and kicks him out of the house. He spends the rest of his life miserably, 'with fifty others, whose stories were not much different' (p. 335), in an old men's home. Loyal himself to family feeling, he finds himself rejected by the family when he can be of no more use to it. The self-respecting workingman has been dispossessed by the hungry generations that have followed him. The Cotter family proves far more destructive and far more unhappy than the Pollit family of *The Man Who Loved Children*. Attacked from the outside and disintegrating from within, Cotters' England destroys the dreams of all it touches.

The Little Hotel: Running from doomsday

In the period immediately following World War II, the Hotel Swiss-Touring harbours a miscellaneous collection of permanent tourists, refugees and expatriates. They are fleeing real and imagined dangers: desperate poverty in Italy, if they are servants; financial ruin, if they are guests. The Belgian 'Mayor of B' is running from 'Germans' and the lunatic asylum; the English are fleeing a Labour government at home and the collapse of their Empire abroad; an American from the South wishes to avoid 'racial contamination'; and everyone is trying to second-guess the newest symbol of doom, the Russians. Among the servants, hostilities are continually breaking out between the French and the Italians and between the Swiss-French and Swiss-Germans. As Europe enters the Cold War this little hotel represents, as if in microcosm, the ambiance of the times.

Everyone is running from doomsday but no one is sure where safety may be found. Many see South America as their next great hope, because 'your money is safe with a dictator. He keeps the greedy people down . . . .'[4] Princess

Bili is investing in a face-lift. Robert Wilkins puts his faith in his financial charts. His unacknowledged mistress of 27 years, Mrs Trollope, has put all hers in their great love. Her off and on friend, Mrs Blaise, has turned to drugs. And Mrs Blaise's sinister husband, the doctor, believes only in doomsday itself: 'doomsday always comes', laughs the doctor, 'with a sidelong glance towards his wife' (p. 134). His chilling prediction comes true for them at least: by the end of the novel it is apparent, although never stated outright, that he has succeeded in killing his wife and gaining her fortune for himself.

The story of their miserable marriage parallels that of the end of the affair between Mr Wilkins and Mrs Trollope. Both men are angling for control of the women's money and seem prepared to go to any lengths to get it, Mr Wilkins gaily hinting at a car accident that he thinks unlikely only because unnecessary: Mrs Trollope has already put him 'at the wheel of her fortune' of her own free will (pp. 125–26). Their relationship now may be summed up in a single exchange: ' "We are one flesh," she had said to him, with deep emotion. "And one fortune," he said quickly, embarrassed' (p. 158). She knows he is trying to 'swallow' her fortune, telling Princess Bili: 'now that he is not in business he wants to make money out of me' (p. 161). Rapacity is a habit not easily lost. The business instinct must find an outlet somewhere, and for a mentality accustomed to thinking of everything in terms of property, it is a logical step to see one's lover in the same terms. Malaya, the colony, is no longer available for exploitation: Mr Wilkins turns to Lilia, the woman he found there, as the next best thing. Yet for them it had once been a genuine love affair, as it had never been for the Blaises. Dr Blaise 'came from a hungry farm' (p. 122) and cold-bloodedly married a fortune. They had never loved. In contrast, Robert and Lilia had been happy in Malaya. But that tropical happiness cannot survive in the winds of

Cold War Europe. Although Robert has his own money
and does not need hers, he has grown more anxious,
smallminded, grasping and prejudiced since his return
'home'. The issue of race, especially, a non-issue in Malaya,
suddenly appears to be an important consideration in race-
conscious Europe.

This is one of the great ironies of the postwar period.
The Little Hotel shows that although the Nazis lost the war,
their most pernicious theories survived it quite well. Because
Mrs Trollope's mother was a Dutch-Javanese, Mr Wilkins'
family refer to her as 'that half-caste', he will not marry
her, the American Mrs Powell calls her 'that Asiatic' and
even her supposed friend Mrs Blaise (obviously a Nazi
sympathiser who has money stolen from Nazis invested in
the United States and who believes that the 'Germans lost
the war owing to the intervention of the Jews' [p. 31])
secretly and even openly despises her because she is 'not
white'.

Racism goes hand in hand with other kinds of intolerance.
Those most fearful of racial contamination – even from the
mere presence of Negroes in the same dining room – are
those most fearful of communist infiltration. Ironically, the
very Americans who 'won the war against Fascism' are
now the characters most violently expressing these views.
Mrs Powell, the 'most exaggerated American' the
hotelkeeper has ever known, explains the connection
between racial mixing and communism at some
length:

Darwin showed that God has arranged it so that blood
will tell . . . . No one would approve of Hitler, but he
understood the danger . . . . Now I cannot approve of
the extermination of peoples and yet you might say he
was like a surgeon cutting out the disease . . . .
Everywhere you turn, in every street, almost in every
hotel, in this hotel, you will find some of them. But it's

unworkable. It will break down. Our culture will break down and the Russians come in. (p. 38)

Mrs Powell distributes pamphlets claiming that Marx 'was a revolutionary because of his liver trouble' (p. 40). As part of her campaign to get rid of Mrs Trollope, she remarks to one of the servants, in Mrs Trollope's hearing, 'I never imagined there would be so many coloured people and half-breeds about in Switzerland. Communism attracts such unfortunates' (p. 54). And on another occasion complains: 'There are communists even in this country, in Switzerland. Why don't you get busy and stand them all up against the wall?' (p. 17). Most of the guests agree with her that this would be a good idea. The hotelkeeper concludes, in her deadpan way: 'She was the most patriotic American I ever met' (p. 54).

The entire novel (except for the odd, careless slip) emerges in this hotelkeeper's voice, as one long monologue addressed in a familiar manner to a 'you' – perhaps Stead herself – who also knows the hotel. For example, of a businessman who tries to cheat her, she remarks: 'You may have noticed him in the dining-room' (p. 9). This imagined narrative context lends intimacy and a gossipy tone to her narrative. Recently Patricia Meyer Spacks has devoted a carefully researched study to the rehabilitation of the reputation of gossip as a peculiarly female and valuable narrative art form.[5] In *The Little Hotel*, Stead provides fuel for Spacks' argument. People confide in Selda. Talk helps them work through their problems and, as Mrs Trollope observes, Selda understands 'people without criticizing them' (p. 186); that is part of her job. But she too needs a friend with whom she can share secrets. Hence the genesis of *The Little Hotel*. Selda rambles on apparently at random, but her artless style reveals underlying patterns formed by illusion and disillusion, trust and betrayal, love and money

that convey a carefully constructed vision of the world that
is recognisably Stead's.

In this vision, no detail is too small to escape her notice,
because each contributes to the design of the whole.
Individual human lives are inextricably involved in the
temper of their times, both contributing to their shape and
being shaped by them in turn. The end of a love affair may
be a universal theme, but the way in which Mrs Trollope's
love dies, and even the angle from which we view it dying,
are particular to this specific time and place. Their dying
love reflects the dying power of the British Empire to
hold disparate peoples together; it reveals the financial
underpinning, the self-interest, of a supposedly philan-
thropic undertaking. Just as the Dutch lady believes that
the 'backward peoples . . . need us to find the way out for
them' (p. 37), so Mr Wilkins believes that Lilia, a mere
woman, although excellent at figures, cannot manage her
own affairs. He tells himself he is appropriating Lilia's
fortune 'for her own good', holding on to it, against her
will, even after she has left him, 'for her sake' (p. 189).
Like Mrs Powell, he convinces himself of his good
intentions, but he cannot convince us.

The indirect style of Stead's narration gives her readers
the pleasure of seeing more than her characters see.
Through the filter of Selda's sharp observations, clear
patterns emerge; but because she herself is an actor as well
as an observer of the action, even she cannot see everything
with the detachment the reader brings. She has her own
worries about her husband's fidelity that colour her
perceptions of others. For her, 'when you grow up and
marry, there is a shadow over everything' (p. 7). Between
Selda and her girlfriend, there had been no secrets. Now,
however, she cannot discuss her anxieties with her husband.
Because she is afraid of what she might discover, there is a
permanent gap between them. The novel's first anecdote,
of the mysterious phone calls from Geneva, sets the tone

for what follows. Selda senses that over everything said in these endless phone calls hangs the weight of something that cannot be said, 'there was something weighing on her which she could not tell me' (p. 8). When the crisis comes, its content is blurred. The more Selda narrates, the more uncertain she becomes. There is confusion on both ends of the line, compounded by language difficulties, and finally it seems that Selda's discretion will not allow her to know too much: the mystery remains. The same thing happens with the Mayor of B. Who he really is, why he behaves as he does, where he goes – all remain unanswerable mysteries. Miss Chillard, too, hides a history that no one penetrates. And the final words of the novel, referring to Lilia and Robert, explain 'I do not know if they ever saw each other again' (p. 191).

The cumulative effect of so much hanging unsaid, behind the impenetrable stream of talk that is the substance of the novel, creates the pathos of the transient lives that fill the little hotel. There is plenty of violence and drama here but it is disconnected from a past or a future. We see as Selda does, a mere fragment of a life as it passes through on its way somewhere else, or as Mrs Trollope does, watching everything in the reflecting mirror of the dining room, while Mr Wilkins ignores her to read his paper. If Cotters' England is trapped in the hall of distorting mirrors created by its history of poverty and misplaced patriotism, then the life of the little hotel is trapped in a different mirror, reflecting the empty lives of those who have too little to do. Lilia complains of watching 'this sad lot of scarecrows that we are, in the mirror' (p. 153). In their fears of commitment, they have emptied themselves of humanity until they are nothing but scarecrows, reflections of human beings trapped in the wandering lives they have shaped for themselves as defences. Just as *A Little Tea, a Little Chat* shows the seducer seduced and *Cotters' England* the deceiver self-deceived so *The Little Hotel* shows those running from doomsday creating it in themselves. In Stead's view, the punishment always fits the crime because people fashion for themselves the fate that ultimately consumes them. Hers is an increasingly grim view of humanity. No one escapes the cruel revelations of the mirror of her fiction, not even the innocuous victims like Mrs Trollope.

But it would be a mistake to see Stead as a misanthrope, like Dr Blaise, who says: 'I am a satirist of human nature, of which I have the worst opinion' (p. 133). The worship of force, the toadying to power, is all he sees or knows. Stead sees what he sees, but she also sees what he misses – the delight in incongruities, the humour in discrepancies, the occasional genuinely disinterested act. Nothing is too horrible to surprise Dr Blaise. Even evil bores him. But everything surprises Stead. Because nothing bores her, nothing she presents to her readers can bore them. In all her work, Stead seems to feel as Selda does, that even when you understand someone's story, 'you are always astonished at how people can muddle their lives' (p. 19). That astonishment prevents despair by seeing freshness in the stalest stories and humour in what to the participants is deadly earnest. And while people persist in muddling their lives, they are capable of clarifying them too. Leaving Robert to retreat on his own into a 'dream-world' where cards alone absorb him, Lilia strikes out for herself in search of more meaningful work, happy at last to shed her debilitating dependency and make her own independent life.

As in many Stead novels, a dinner scene encapsulates the options facing the inhabitants of the little hotel. What was designed to be the celebration of the miraculous first meeting of two people discovering that they loved one another, degenerates into a sordid scene of exploitation masterminded by the leeching Blaises. Greedily ordering all the most expensive dishes, not for the pleasure of the food but merely to humiliate their hosts, they represent humanity at its worst: bickering, ostentatious and vicious. The obscene photographs of hideous diseases that Mrs Blaise insists on distributing about the table reinforce Stead's point that this is a diseased society she is depicting. All the talk revolves about how much these people hate one another and how much they love and need their money. The absurd singing dog provides the final touch. Yet she is no more distorted than her human companions. Sensing that something has gone terribly wrong, Lilia takes refuge in the dominant clichés of the time: 'I call it a very cruel age; I never know where to turn. It is the communists who have driven us so far out of our old ways of thinking, and the blame is on them . . . . After all, they set the pace; we are all hag-ridden' (p. 131). As Selda charitably observes of her guests in general: 'People who do nothing for a number of years are naturally eccentric' (p. 27). Too much leisure can addle the brain. When people like Lilia find their lives of unending conspicuous consumption too tedious to bear, they find it more convenient to blame the communists than to examine their own lives. Or they turn to more and more sophisticated games of cruelty like the Blaises. The drama of this anniversary dinner, gone so horribly wrong, represents the malaise of the Cold War period. These are the people George Cotter refers to, when he speaks of 'their England' in opposition to 'Cotters' England'. 'They' can afford to run from the supposed doomsday of a Labour government at home to gilded exile in a European hotel, but escape eludes them as surely as it does the Cotters. The little hotel proves no alternative to Cotters' England.

Miss Herbert (The Suburban Wife): Unawakened Venus

Miss Herbert is the final volume of Stead's trilogy on postwar Britain. After the poverty of Cotters' England and the haunted leisure of expatriate England comes the cramping respectability of suburban England. Again the focus is on a woman's unconscious experience of the limitations of her class. Eleanor Herbert Brent, like most Stead characters, remains a self-deluded egotist, but of a type never highlighted before in Stead's work. She is the quintessential 'suburban wife', in mentality if not in actual fact, since her husband deserts her and the children, unable to stand so much perfection according to the tenets laid down in the housewives' magazines that dictate Eleanor's life. This gap between the ideal and the real remains the chief puzzle for Eleanor throughout her story. At its end, she accepts the fact that 'I kept to the rules, but the rules didn't keep me';[6] but she still cannot understand how her plans went wrong. The reader, however, sees what Eleanor does not want to see: that the rules put women in a double-bind situation which turns even 'success' into failure.

Nonetheless, Eleanor lives the life she has chosen to live. Preferring security to adventure, 'fresh air' to 'passion' as she puts it in deciding to reject Edward Thieme (p. 73), Eleanor avoids all challenges to her suburban sense of self. Occasionally she feels that she is missing something but she never dares to find out what. The novel is built around two voids: the essential emptiness of Eleanor's superficially busy suburban life and the mystery she is afraid to acknowledge, her own capacity for passionate self-abandon.

The unlived life of the suburbanite could prove dreary reading indeed. Stead makes it interesting, and not simply for itself alone, but as an indication of the ruling illusions of the period during which Eleanor's life takes place. Like the 'puzzleheaded girls' of Stead's novellas, she lives through a great deal while remaining essentially untouched by most of what happens to her. Amnesia proves a convenient solution for reconciling society's ideas of the proper behaviour of a 'lady' with her own experiments in what she thinks of as 'low life' during the twenties and thirties. Eleanor has perfected her capacity for self-deception to the extent that she can not only deny her past but also live a double life in the present, without feeling at all hypocritical. The kind of 'doublespeak' Orwell predicted for 1984 already existed in his own society, as Eleanor's experience shows. Her fear of involvement in love, in a relationship with one other human being, parallels her fear of involvement in political activity, in the assuming of a communal responsibility.

The novel's opening scene demonstrates how women, in particular, develop protective strategies to cope with their society's contradictory demands upon them. Although marriage seems to have faded all their friends, these single women, who are vigorously alive and working in their chosen careers, still feel they should wish to marry. Although fighting for their right to define themselves, they still find it difficult to free themselves completely. Eleanor, a beauty who wants to be taken seriously, already unconsciously lives a double life. With women, she feels at ease and says what she thinks. With men, she says 'what she thought correct, depending on her textbooks, afraid to accept any idea that she had no authority for' (p. 5). Yet even when Eleanor is being herself, her upbringing and the dominant values of her class speak through her. The will to please is so deeply ingrained in her nature that it leads her to avoid controversy at any cost, and to mistake her own interests.

Her rejection of Tom Dickon, her first fiancé, reveals a complacent willingness to uphold the status quo even when it operates against her own happiness. Eleanor echoes the establishment view when she dismisses Tom's political commitment by reducing it to an individual psychological problem: 'He had a will to fail' (p. 6). Dr Mack, however, believes that Tom was trying to change his society before it could change him. To Eleanor such thinking is inconceivable: she can only repeat that Tom is 'weak'. But the story itself supports Dr Mack's interpretation. The University Senate had expelled Tom, one of their most promising students, for marching in a May Day parade, which ended in a brawl with the police. Most of the women think Eleanor was right to return the ring as soon as Tom came out of prison, but one expresses the radical idea that 'a girl ought to stand by her fiancé in trouble', earning Eleanor's belittling comment: 'Dear little Vina, our gallant little extremist' (p. 7). Ironically, the language Eleanor uses here to discredit her friend's ideas without engaging them is precisely the same kind of language used by men to dismiss women. This connection is made explicit when another woman adds: 'But suppose he did it for what he thought right? . . . My mother was in jail as a suffragette'. Their black and white world of right and wrong breaks down when confronted with actual experience, but none of these women wishes to follow where such thoughts might lead them. Eleanor, in particular, works hard at closing her mind to complexities and wins prizes at school for her success. But at the end of the novel she is puzzled, defeated by life. She feels as if she had fallen into a cold crevasse in Tibet and never fully recovered. In contrast, Dr Mack has actually gone to Tibet, where she 'is trying to get to the forbidden territory' (p. 307).

Unlike Linda Mack, Eleanor prides herself on being a 'normal' woman, accepting the goals her society has prescribed for her: 'I want to marry and have my own home and have my children and then I want to be a person in my own right!' (p. 12). *Miss Herbert* explores the dimensions of a life devoted to the pursuit of such aims. Believing in true individualist fashion that the pursuit of her own happiness must coincide with society's good, Eleanor acts as she pleases. Long before Helen Gurley Brown's *Sex and the Single Girl*, Eleanor lived the lifestyle of a 'Cosmopolitan girl', mistaking promiscuity for liberation. An argument with her teacher, Mrs Appleyard, who is a genuine feminist, reveals Eleanor's confusion: 'You can't say the sexual act is black one time and white another. Either it's wrong or it's right. Where's your logic, Apple? Love is respect and sex is lust' (p. 30). Despite all her acquaintances whose lives disprove this formula, she adopts it unquestioningly from her mother's teaching and never escapes the straitjacket it imposes on her own sex life.

Believing that 'a single girl must lead a double life' (p. 25), she keeps her chaste engagement with Robert completely separate from her numerous 'flings' with other men. She thinks Robert can only respect her if she refuses to make love with him; and that what she does with other men is irrelevant to her relationship with him because it is 'sex' not 'love'. Although her reasoning seems perverse, it results from a literal reading of the instructions her society gives women of her class. When love and sex are seen as incompatible, a double standard is bound to result. This double standard enables Eleanor to see herself as both a 'Wife of Bath' and 'irreversibly a lady' no matter what she does (p. 24). So strongly does she believe that her society is on her side, that she feels betrayed when Robert develops a real relationship with another woman. He has broken the rules of their game, by bringing sexual attraction and love together.

Ironically, Eleanor's separation of the two allows her no pleasure. Sex not only becomes sterile when separated from love, but often so close to a merely commercial transaction as to make her feel shamed. Conversely, love without sex also becomes a degraded and empty parody of the real thing in Eleanor's experience. Like the first story she writes, her life becomes more and more barren as she prunes it to conform to the rules she has extracted from various manuals on how to write. The more she rewrites the story according to formula, the more miserably it fails.

But she plods on, telling herself: 'I follow the rules, I am bound to win' (p. 22). Similarly, Eleanor's obsessive concern with the proprieties only serves to make her more vulgar. Granting herself a clear conscience by virtue of her 'doublethinking', she prys prudishly into the lives of her friends who live unified lives according to a single standard of value. She sees Marky and Diana, who live openly with their lovers, Ivo and Thomas, as 'scarlet women' because they refuse to marry. Her own stream of lovers who come with letters of introduction and pay her for her services in gifts or meals are allowable because they have no social recognition and do not challenge the established order. Eleanor feels proud that men are attracted to her, failing to recognise that she is being used, and that her own behaviour merely contributes to the continuing marginalisation of her sex. Although she has a university education, her thinking remains bounded by the sentimental clichés she has learned from her mother, described as a 'sweet sawdust' woman, and the trashy magazines she reads in the hope of learning how to write for money.

But her sentimentality does not completely mask some shrewd common sense. It is just that both, as Eleanor understands them, encourage her to mistrust her own instincts. Whereas Jane Austen had contrasted the qualities of 'sense' and 'sensibility', embodying each in a different heroine to valorise 'sense', Stead understands that the English middle class of the twentieth century mistake sentiment for sensibility, allying it with sense to drive out passion and with it any hope of a meaningful, fully human existence. The night before Eleanor's wedding she realises: 'I am to marry a man I don't love', and she wonders: 'How had it happened?' (p. 85). Eleanor's justification lies in her belief that 'There is sentiment in it and sense too'. For sense and sentiment she ignores her aching heart. Yet she feels 'flustered and anxious, as if about to walk with a meek willing crowd into a prison: She had made a fatal promise in a dream and was only now waking up'. The metaphors suggest that our civilisation's tendency to value reason above passion have led us seriously astray, into a prison of our own making. Eleanor is not alone in trying to run her life according to a rational, approved plan that equates financial security with happiness and makes no allowances for emotional growth. While Eleanor usually thinks passion a dangerous dream from which one must awaken to the realities of everyday existence, here she instinctively sees what the entire novel suggests – that everyday life is the sleep from which this Venus must awaken if she is ever to find herself. But unlike Teresa, Eleanor is a Venus in flight from Cythera. Twice she nearly awakens, but each time refuses the voyage.

The language used for Eleanor's brushes with the passion that could have saved her from mediocrity suggests that conventional notions of self must be annihilated before true self-realisation can occur. The first 'meaningless but profound and moving look' she exchanges with Thieme arouses thoughts of death, emptiness and love (p. 43), while recalling the intensity of her first involvement with Tom. It is Thieme who calls her a 'Venus unknown to Venus' (p. 60) and 'the most unawakened woman' he has ever met (p. 61) after she rejects his love, saying she dislikes the 'disorderly feeling' he gives her; she believes in 'self control'. Her second intimation of what she has missed comes when she meets her daughter's suitor, Paul Waters. For the first time, this life she has never known attracts her almost as much as it repels her, but again she rejects it, thinking: 'I would lose myself; I'd be swept away; I don't want that' (p. 304). The novel's centre of value resides in these two moments: they suggest the potential Eleanor fails to realise. Like Louisa Pollit, out of chaos she might have made a dancing star; like Teresa Hawkins, she might have made the voyage to Cythera. Instead, she chooses, like Letty Fox, to conform to what her society expects of her. Whereas *Letty Fox* explores why a woman might choose to make such an apparently unrewarding choice, *Miss Herbert* explores the consequences of making such a decision.

Unlike Letty, Eleanor cannot delude herself into falling in love with each of her transient lovers. Instead, all her love affairs are extensions of her narcissistic fascination with the perfection of her own body, which she likes to see others admiring but which she does not know how to enjoy. For her, Mr Quaideson proves the ideal lover. A man who has perfected the art of living vicariously, sucking life from the antique instruments of torture with which he surrounds himself, he makes her pose for him, but never touches her. Stead describes convincingly the dilemma of a beautiful woman, raised to think of herself as a 'ripe peach' (p. 16) for men's enjoyment at the same time as she is meant to be a person 'in her own right'. For most women, sexuality begins in narcissism. They see their bodies everywhere depicted as sexually exciting. The erotic traditions they have inherited have been almost entirely male-defined. Some women, like Letty, learn to see men as sexually beautiful too; but many, like Eleanor, find such a concept too disconcerting. Thieme offers her this possibility. When she sees him, she thinks involuntarily what men have always said of her: 'What a beauty!' (p. 44). It is precisely this quality in Thieme that she finds most unnerving, for it would force her out of her easy passivity into unfamiliar action. A marriage with Thieme would have required giving as well as taking.

Heinrich Charles proposes in terms more consonant with Eleanor's way of thinking, asking for 'equity' rather than 'love'. Both wish to begin marriage with a 'clean slate' (p. 78), cutting themselves off from their old friends because they think of marriage as a new business venture. A 'modern' woman, Eleanor wants a planned life, organised according to reason. Tired of her aimless affairs, Eleanor thinks: 'I must marry and then life will be an open book, not chewed-over stories from magazines' (p. 73). The metaphor is revealing. In a manner typical of her muddled thinking, the choice she poses herself here is an illusory one. The simplicity of the 'open book' conforms to the simplicity of the 'chewed-over story': like Eleanor, both avoid the mystery of true passion.

Another of Stead's memorable dinner parties reveals the emptiness of the marriage built on such principles. The frugal engagement party Eleanor gives for her au pair girl is both funny and sad in the way it shows clichés colliding with reality. Eleanor has forgotten how to think except in quotations from her modest magazines. She loses her temper when her guests fail to conform to plan, actually starting to enjoy themselves and to eat and drink beyond the stingy measures she has allowed them. And she cannot understand her husband's fury at her lack of flexibility. The increasing gap between the barren reality of her marriage and her rosy mythologising of it prepares the reader for other holes in Eleanor's version of the world.

Eleanor's life story proves the argument put forward by her father, brother and sister-in-law to counter her apolitical complacency. In opposition to Eleanor, they insist that theirs is 'not a perfectly free society, that covert understandings had repressed thoughts and thoughts had dwindled and died' (p. 131). But as usual, Eleanor hardly bothers to listen to what they say. Hers is the typical liberal stance: 'I agree with you all, up to a point', which translated means, as her brother laughingly puts it: 'Well, in short, grin and bear it' (p. 132). Yet her own experience runs increasingly counter to the maxims she mouths. She feels she has been a textbook perfect wife, and her husband discards her. Under English law, her 'work and money' belong to a stranger she married (p. 134). Even she can see that she is very badly paid for the freelance editorial work she does. As a fifty-year-old woman with the experience of a housewife she hasn't a chance of getting a job, even in times of full employment. The evidence increasingly contradicts her vision of the world, but she cannot change her views without losing her only sustaining vision of herself.

Her marriage breaks down as peace and the status of the Empire erode before the rise of Nazi Germany. For her at this time 'national and personal troubles were all one' (p. 164). In her bleakest moments, she entertains the questions: 'What if we go down? If it's all been for nothing? If we've all been wrong?' (p. 165). But more often she retreats into wilful blindness, rejecting the evidence of Nazi aggression in the same way she rejects the evidence of her marriage's disintegration. Like Nellie Cotter, she personalises everything in order to minimalise its challenge to conventional habits of thought. Eleanor does 'not hold with "bogey" talk of fascism renascent. Fascism is not people' (p. 166). And she is appalled by the impropriety of the thought that a Resistance movement might be formed in Britain if the country were to fall to the Germans: 'The proper thing would be to do your work and say nothing', she tells her brother (p. 167). When her self-confidence in British superiority is undermined, Eleanor resorts to the same scapegoating strategies as the Nazi 'enemy', but without meaning any harm or even realising exactly what she is doing. As a literary editor, she applies the same principles of unthinking prejudice to the manuscripts she reads, arguing that 'To put politics into writing is to mix the eternal values with bits and pieces of topical ideas and temporary greeds' (p. 244). For Eleanor, the 'eternal' values translate into her own inherited values.

Stead's greatest strength lies in her systematic exposure of the illogicality of such thinking, while understanding exactly how and why people cling to its illusory comfort. Eleanor's story records the wasting of potential, the frustrating of desire, the distortion of personality, that is a far more common feature of our society than are the rare success stories that are used to justify its existence. Eleanor's gender determines the particular shape and tone of her failure but is not integral to the basic story of her selling of her human birthright for a mess of pottage. She meets many women who with much less promising beginnings have succeeded where she has failed, and numerous men who live as she does, Grub Street hacks who have abandoned their integrity to play it safe. Yet her gender does mean that the mere struggle to make a living – despite her willingness to do anything – remains tougher for her than for the men she knows. And because her struggle is more bitter, her mere survival seems a victory of a kind. As usual with Stead, Eleanor lives most poignantly through her voice – a distressingly funny amalgam of literary tags and crude clichés. She literally has no words of her own. Yet the mishmash she speaks becomes unmistakably her and a telling condemnation of the values that speak through her.

Miss Herbert demonstrates how every aspect of our society has been organised to put women in a double-bind situation. Ignorance and silliness are officially encouraged as proper behaviour for the 'normal' woman which Eleanor aspires to be; these same traits are then used to justify the marginalisation of the women who adopt them. Most of Eleanor's friends avoid the problem by ignoring official rhetoric and getting on with their lives. Eleanor takes it seriously, only to discover that men do not really want to marry silly, prudish wives that they can 'respect' nor do people really want to hire a proper 'lady' with experience managing a household. In the employment agency, she realises that the life she had been proud of looks empty to others. Here she shows the strength underlying her flighty social self. Looking at herself in the glass, she thinks: 'I look old-fashioned, fussy, a suburban wife and mother, but I've got somehow to get out of myself and get a job, in spite of age and looks' (p. 265). Unable to find anyone to hire her, she starts her own small business and after years of struggle makes it a success.

Her youthful beauty has yielded to a new face, coarse, 'heavy, but strong and real' (p. 306). After all her chameleon-like attempts to adapt to her successive environments, Eleanor seems to accept herself as she is in old age. Ironically, the discarding of her illusions ages her even as it gives her a new dignity. True to her lifelong pattern of fleeing a challenge, she retreats from the emotions Paul Watson has awakened in her into the approved role of a grandmotherly figure who has moved beyond sex. Throughout Eleanor's life, Stead shows not only how the conventional roles for women constrain and distort the instincts, but also that the safety they appear to offer is illusory. *Miss Herbert* tells the story of a promising life that betrays its promise, not dramatically as in a classical tragedy, but slowly, almost imperceptibly, step by step over a lifetime. The 'mature acceptance of her fate' that Eleanor believes she has come to, and that a Leavisite critic might approve, is I believe belied by the action of the novel as a whole, which suggests that this mellow conclusion can only be seen as yet another, final sell out.

The greatness of *Miss Herbert* lies in the way it helps us to see that Eleanor's betrayal of herself is not merely a personal betrayal but part of a larger compromise on the part of Western peoples in general. 'Hewing to the line' and 'cultivating one's garden' are not enough. They lead to the acceptance of all kinds of atrocities in the name of keeping the peace, to sterility and to fear. As Louisa tells Sam in *The Man Who Loved Children*, to oppose chaos to order is to misdraw the boundaries that define our lives. Eleanor chooses repression and death, mistaking them for peace, rather than the turbulence of passionate endeavour, which she associates with anarchy. But as her story shows, Eleanor's conventionally 'ordered' life is the truly anarchic one, whereas her brother's unconventional but principled life generates its own internally coherent order.

In *Miss Herbert*, Stead exposes the mediocrity of a middle class in love with its own limitations just as in *Cotters' England* she exposes the defeatism of a working class in love with its victimisation. In each case, wilful ignorance and its companion, an unthinking acceptance of the status quo, are the villains. The answers are harder to define. Both Nellie and Eleanor go through life feeling that they have missed something, that there is a key to a mystery they cannot unlock with the ideas that they have embraced. The novels employ the metaphor of passionate love to suggest that mystery – a surrender of the self to something other than oneself, to vulnerability, to caring – a surrender that connects one to the world in a relation that is mutually supportive rather than exploitative. Paradoxically, while the idea of such a love is frightening, the reality eliminates fear. This is a disconcerting metaphor for several reasons. Women have traditionally been trained to seek self-realisation in a romantic relationship with a man rather than through paid work in the larger community. Surely Stead cannot be advocating this private solution, originally employed to keep women content in their exclusion from power, as a solution for all her characters. The consistently iconoclastic treatment of romantic notions in all her books would seem to rule out such a reading. For Stead, 'romance' is not 'love'. Romance upholds the present inequitable order; love destroys it.

Love destroys, as does all genuine creativity, through questioning. As Teresa recognises, love is not blind. On the contrary, it sees so clearly as to cause discomfort with things as they are. Heterosexual love breaks down the traditional boundaries between the divided experiences of the two sexes. Their artificial social separation begins to look ridiculous. When their own experience contradicts their cultural training in this sphere, people begin to question it in other spheres as well. *For Love Alone* articulates the beginning of this process, linking sexual liberation to the liberation of the community as a whole. Tom and Marion in *Cotters' England* and George and Madge (amongst others) in *Miss Herbert* continue this process in the background of texts that are more centrally concerned with the conservative forces opposing change than directly with their overthrow. With the revival of capitalism during the postwar period, Stead made a strategic decision, paralleled by the choices of the new feminist critics, to analyse the forces of repression rather than try to imagine what might replace them in our lives. Marx rewrote economics, but the rewriting of conventional habits of thought and belief, of what are now often referred to as ideologies, took much longer to materialise. Stead's fiction plays an important role in that rewriting. Her vision is as far from orthodox Marxist social realism as it is from conventional bourgeois realism. It casts an independently cold eye over the self-delusions of all.

8 Stead and her Critics

Christina Stead's novels have been misunderstood by some and ignored, until recently, by many. As the passing of time puts her period into perspective we can understand more clearly why her reception has been so uneven. This study argues that she formulated her political concerns in terms of metaphors of love – the voyage to Cythera made by the awakened Venus and its opposite, the voyage refused by the unawakened Venus. This metaphor challenges conventional understandings of love and politics, breaking down the boundaries between public and private that much acclaimed English fiction had carefully established. As time passes it should become easier to see the ways in which many of Stead's characters function as 'world-historical individuals' in the Lukácsian sense of that term. Stead's fiction belongs to the great tradition of European realism analysed by Lukács rather than to the great tradition of the English novel identified by Leavis. Stead wrote the history of her experience of the major periods of the twentieth century – from the twenties to the fifties – as an involved participant who saw those times within the framework of a materialist analysis. Aware of the increasingly hostile reception such an analysis could expect from the readers of the time, she displaced it from the level of explicit commentary to enact it indirectly through patterns of metaphor and play with irony. But whether she wrote of the social ferment of the twenties and

thirties, the threat and impact of war in the forties or the
'moral bottom' of the fifties, her writing drew attention to
the ideological constraints – otherwise as invisible as the air
we breathe – that continually frustrate genuine social
change.

For many years, Christina Stead was a writer who earned
mixed reviews for novels that were allowed to go out of
print. In 1955 Elizabeth Hardwick published an article on
'The Neglected Novels of Christina Stead', deploring the
fact that at that time, fifteen years after the *The Man Who
Loved Children* had appeared to critical praise, none of
Stead's work remained in print.[1] The postwar years were
the least sympathetic to Stead's iconoclastic vision.
Hardwick's attempt at a Stead revival failed. Ten years
later the critical climate was more favourable. Randall
Jarrell's enthusiastic introduction to the reissue of *The Man
Who Loved Children* in the United States in 1965 and in
England in 1966 coincided with a wave of reprints. In
Australia *Seven Poor Men of Sydney*, *For Love Alone* and
The Salzburg Tales were reissued. As the novels became
available, academics began teaching them on Australian
literature courses and critical material started to appear.
Now for the first time ever all of Stead's work is readily
available to her readers.

This revival reflects the shift in critical temper away
from modernism's search for order in art that conformed
to Cleanth Brooks' ideal – 'the well-shaped urn' – toward
post-modernism's fascination with open-ended forms.
Literary feminism's movement away from a search for
positive role models in fiction toward more sophisticated
analyses of the pressures of gender on voice, style and
structure within texts also benefited Stead. Academic
Marxism's explorations of the ideological participations of
literary texts, as begun by Althusser and continued by
Macherey and Eagleton, have suggested approaches more
fruitful than those of socialist realism to the complexities of

Stead's fiction. Reappraisals of her work are now in full swing.

In 1967 the literature committee of the Britannica Australia Award had recommended that Stead be granted the $10 000 literature prize for that year but the council rejected the nomination on the grounds that her long absence from Australia had rendered her ineligible. While Stead's expatriation may well have contributed to her neglect in Australia, other factors have influenced her reception there and abroad. Many felt that the Britannica decision reflected deeper political issues than that of residence. In the aftermath of the Cold War, her political sympathies were not likely to make her popular with the establishment. As Stead pointed out the next year, in explaining her youthful impulse to compile an Encyclopaedia of Obscure People as a counter Who's Who: 'I knew something about official reference books and I knew some very able people who would never appear there, because of their beliefs.'[2] Stead herself cared little for these external accolades awarded by an establishment whose values she questioned. She strove to meet her own standards, of truth to the material as she saw it.

Stead's gender was first raised as yet another factor contributing to her neglect in 1973 when Anne Summers published her pioneering article on 'The Self Denied: Australian Women Writers – Their Image of Women'. Summers argued that 'The revolutionary honours' that went to Patrick White for changing the face of Australian fiction 'should have gone to Christina Stead; as an expatriate and a woman, she appears to have forfeited the right to be recognised as contributing to national literary traditions.'[3] Summers' assessment of Stead's achievement if not her explanation for Stead's neglect has become the new orthodoxy in Australia. Stead now receives the 'revolutionary honours' initially denied her. Even unsympathetic critics, such as Adrian Mitchell in the much criticised *Oxford*

History of Australian Literature, feel obliged to acknowledge her stylistic innovations while continuing to misunderstand her greatness.

It seems less clear, however, that Stead's neglect can be ascribed to her gender – unless we see her diffidence about seeking publicity as deriving from her training in female role behaviour and her unusual narrative structures as deriving from her specifically female experience. Her lack of assertiveness in twice allowing her publishers to give her novels misleading titles has contributed to misunderstanding of her work. Both *For Love Alone* and *Dark Places of the Heart*, the two externally imposed titles, conform to stereotypes of the woman's romantic novel that are not met by the novels themselves. As a woman with socialist values. Stead does not seem to have felt the exclusive property rights in her creations that Harold Bloom in *The Anxiety of Influence* associates with the capitalist male literary tradition. She stated many times that she did not care what happened to her books once they were written. The process of writing engrossed all her energies. She had little time for promoting the finished product.

While some male critics' objections to her work seem related to their own gender-specific expectations, others seem to have been able to transcend those limitations to enter sympathetically into her vision. Indeed, some of Stead's most perceptive – as well as enthusiastic critics – happen to be men and some of her most hostile reviews have come from women.[4]

Unlike writing by some women writers, Stead's fiction pleases or angers both sexes in ways that make it difficult to divide the critical response along gender lines alone. Stead herself credited her friend Stanley Burnshaw with initiating Jarrell's revival of *The Man Who Loved Children* and her husband William Blake with engineering her first publication. She appointed Ron Geering her executor. Professor Geering wrote the first two extended critical studies of her work, both published in 1969, and has edited a special issue of her unpublished writings for the journal *Southerly*, a collection of her stories previously published in scattered journals and a text of her unpublished novel *I'm Dying Laughing*.[5]

In a letter to *Partisan Review*, composed in answer to a request to write about the Women's Movement, Stead records her abhorrence of 'any sort of segregation' making a difference between male and female writers but concludes that 'it is not entirely possible at the moment to do the portrait of a woman and present it as such, as it is of a man; it is thought to have a special meaning.'[6] Certainly some Stead criticism persists in seeing her male characters as individuals and her female characters as representatives of their entire sex, in readings the texts themselves expressly forbid but that the prejudices of our society continue to endorse. 'The Family Novel', for example, reads *The Man Who Loved Children* to see Henny as typically female and Sam as triumphantly himself.[7] Some female critics would simply reverse this reading, to see Sam as typically male and Henny as stubbornly herself. Others, like Dorothy Green in 'Storm in a Teacup' insist on Stead's even-handedness in portraying all her characters as individuals. This study has taken the latter approach. Stead's emphasis falls on the shared humanity – rather than on the divisive differences – of the sexes.

The most common readings of Stead that this study has sought to combat are those which bring assumptions to her novels that are bound to be disappointed by her achievement. Critics unsympathetic to the way Stead's vision always roots itself in the political dynamics of a particular time and place tend to deny her realism, asserting instead as Joan Lidoff does that 'her real native land, the country of all her fiction, is the international realm of human fantasy.'[8] American critics in particular seem to need to depoliticise a text before they can enjoy it. In

opposition to Lidoff's reading this study has followed
Terry Sturm in emphasising the originality of Stead's 'new
realism' – a realism that incorporates fantasy without in
any way being escapist.

A careful reading of Christina Stead's fiction exposes the
folly of identifying political awareness – and even political
commitment – with the advocacy of an orthodoxy, whether
it be Marxist or feminist. Stead rejected labels. She did not
see all women as automatically her sisters simply by virtue
of their shared sex. Rather, she assessed all human beings
on the basis of their actions. She refused to recognise
gender as a distinguishing determinant of value and was
distressed when others attempted to judge her work in this
light. After her experience with McCarthyism she also
became wary of political labels. In interviews she was
always evasive, to the point, Angela Carter suggests, of
'acute paranoia'.[9] But this rejection of being categorised too
easily by virtue of her sex or her political beliefs did not
make her a liberal humanist, as some critics have assumed.

Stead was not a propagandist for her beliefs. Although
Stead was undoubtedly influenced by Marxism, Jose
Yglesias overstates her debt when he contends that Marx
was her muse. Stead's antecedents lie in the realism of
European writers like Balzac, Strindberg and the Goncourts.
Like them, she strove to portray honestly the manners she
observed at work in a changing society.

Stead's themes, her method and her characteristic style
are all present in her first novel, *Seven Poor Men of Sydney*.
She did not grow or change so much as expand and
develop the vision revealed there. That vision grew from
late nineteenth- and early twentieth-century conceptions of
human nature and the problems facing the human race.
Stead was intellectually curious and continued to read
widely throughout her life but saw no reason to change the
personal philosophy she had developed after reading
Darwin, Nietzsche, Marx and Balzac. As a result, some of

Stead's assumptions no longer seem as evident to us as they did to her, but the forceful impact of her fiction has not abated. Its energy remains.

The ideological analysis of critics like Terry Sturm and Susan Sheridan (whose early work appears under the name Susan Higgins) seems best adapted to understanding Stead's work. They recognise that Stead is neither a propagandising advocate for a cause nor a liberal humanist who insists on the separation of the private and public worlds. In what Terry Sturm calls Stead's 'new realism', private and public interact because 'ideology is part of the texture of characters' individual lives, inseparable from the way they respond and react to events.'[10] Sheridan puts the case more strongly, to argue that 'ideology *forms* the texture of their *mental* life, which the novelist dramatises in ways which reveal the truths as well as the mystifications inherent in these ideas'.[11] This study follows the lead initiated by Sturm and Sheridan in the belief that Stead's artistry can only be fully appreciated as a dramatisation of the ideological inconsistencies which characterise twentieth-century capitalist society, particularly but not exclusively those which oppress women.

Stead was fifteen when the Russian Revolution occurred. Her high school history class discussed what it might mean. She lived through the years of hope and later of disillusionment that followed on Stalin's assumption of power. She knew first-hand, in Letty Fox's words, that 'you have to keep on fighting for liberty, even in a revolution when you're on the right side'.[12] Lidoff and Geering see Stead's savage portraits of hypocrites, egotists and sell outs on the Left as proof that she is not a political writer, but rather a moral one who focuses on the human character alone, as an entity that can be isolated from time and place. One can only hold such a view if one mistakes blind loyalty to a cause with true political commitment. It is precisely Stead's sophisticated understanding of politics and her commitment to genuine social change that leads her to interrogate the malaise on the Left so incisively. She attacks this target because she supports and cares for the cause, not to provide ammunition for the Right but to help the Left understand its own weaknesses. She never underestimates the dangers from any side – from the declared enemy, the declared supporter (who may sometimes function as an enemy within) or the apathetic middle ground. She cares for truth, not partisanship; equity, not partiality.

A moral emphasis certainly motivates Stead's work but it is far from a conventional or Christian morality. Stead knows right from wrong, but Evil is a concept foreign to her thought. Lidoff seriously misreads Stead when she asserts that 'Stead shares with Christianity a belief in inherent evil . . . .'[13] Stead was not raised a Christian and Christian beliefs are never an issue in her work. Just as Stead's fiction argues that slaves and women are made not born – produced as the social constructs of a society that benefits from their oppression – so she argues that characters act in ways hurtful to themselves and others in reaction to the constraints of their circumstances rather than because of some 'original sin' or 'inherent evil'. Stead's moral vision insists that people remain responsible for their actions while showing us why they sometimes behave destructively. Far from upholding the Christian belief in inherent evil, she reveals that explanation of human behaviour as a convenient fiction masking society's responsibility for the conditions within which it enables its citizens to operate.

Lidoff's attempt to force Stead into an individualistic, Christian framework of belief underestimates the radically original force of Stead's achievement. It also, in Margaret Harris's words, excludes 'most of Stead's politics and much of her intellect'. Harris insists that 'Christina Stead is bigger and tougher than Joan Lidoff makes her'.[14] In a short and focused study such as this one, I can only suggest how much 'bigger and tougher' Stead the writer is, but that has been my aim. Most criticism has underplayed both her socialist values and her wide, even learned range of reading as well as her command of several languages. The early image of Stead as the uncritical and hasty transcriber of the flow of events around her can no longer be maintained when the manuscripts in the Australian National Library so clearly contradict it. Much more work needs to be done on the intertextuality of Stead's fiction, not only to examine the complex interweavings of literary allusion but also her radical rewritings of inherited stories from a woman's perspective. For example, manuscript notes suggest that the Jacky/Gondych affair in *Letty Fox* was conceived as a twentieth-century version of the Faust story with Jacky as 'the new Marguerite'.[15] Clearly a much fuller study of the manuscripts must now begin.

If some critics have trouble with her politics, others are repelled by her style, the natural expression of those politics. Disturbed by her radical revisions of fictional form, some prefer to deny it altogether, seeing her works as 'loose, baggy monsters' of uncontrolled observation and invention. There are some grounds for these objections. Stead's style sometimes sinks beneath its weight of detail. The long list of adjectives which begins *Seven Poor Men of Sydney* tries to say too much too quickly and repels the readers it seeks to attract. Stead's interest lies in telling what she sees, even at the expense of conventional notions of rhythm or beauty. Because she finds language inexact and culturally loaded, she tends to say things in many different ways, attempting through accretion and the interplay of repetition with difference to circumvent inherited assumptions about how language means. We do not read her work for the refining sensibility of a Virginia Woolf, the clarifying moments of revelation of a Katherine Mansfield, the dark expressionism of a Djuna Barnes, the wordplay of a Gertrude Stein, the lyricism of a Jean Rhys, the gothic regionalism of a Eudora Welty, or the mystical politics of a Doris Lessing. She shared neither the high modernist aesthetic nor its style. There are no epiphanies in Stead. There is no sense of art as a new religion nor of the artist as a new priest. Her art provides no refuge from the mundane. Indeed, the mundane is Stead's chosen sphere.

She is the novelist of the worldly – urbane, cosmopolitan, secular. While modernists and social realists alike despised the middle classes and their commercial endeavours as unworthy of any but satiric attention, Stead continued in the nineteenth-century tradition of taking this class seriously as her subject. Stead's fiction centres on the middle-class character. Unlike Lawrence and Woolf, she is not interested in exploring psychological depths nor in questioning what Lawrence termed the 'old stable ego of character'. She begins pragmatically in the belief that most people are what is commonly assumed to be 'normal' and that the novelist can convey the truth of human experience through recording their actions and speech. From a contemporary point of view, which takes nothing – not even beginnings – for granted, this is a serious weakness.

Stead seems to have felt a temperamental distaste for introspection, an impatience with dwelling on the self that resulted from an inability to see such probing as other than narcissistic self-indulgence. Stead's weakest novels, *The Beauties and Furies* and *A Little Tea, a Little Chat*, while not without interest for the Stead enthusiast, seem to have no focus other than to explore – at length – the different egotisms of their central characters in action without ever delving into their personal sources. Because Elvira and Robbie are particularly one-dimensional and not at all charismatic for the reader, their stories are puzzling without being compelling. Stead's refusal to accept Freud saved her work from the misogynist assumptions implicit in psychoanalysis in the middle years of this century but it also turned her writing away from the kind of experiments he was inspiring among her modernist contemporaries. The strength of her approach lies in the equal treatment it affords men and women alike; its weakness, in its failure to probe or question its own initial premises. For the contemporary reader sated with fictional presentations of the dissolution of the personality and the death of the character, it can be refreshing to read of characters who are solidly present as givens, inseparable from the environments in which they are rooted. Stead's old-fashioned view of character is in one sense at least ahead of its times: her refusal to characterise women as victims offers inspiration to critics seeking to go beyond the impasse into which this characterisation, encouraged by patriarchal theory in particular, has led much current feminist thinking.

In Stead's fiction, character is politics. What I claim to be a strength, Adrian Mitchell sees as a fault. He concludes that 'there is in Stead's fiction an imperfect adjustment between inner and outer realities, an interesting misalliance of the novel of character with the novel of ideas'.[16] But Stead does not see inner and outer realities as requiring adjustment; she sees them as seamlessly one. Neither would she separate the 'novel of character' from the 'novel of ideas'. For her there can be no characters without ideas, no ideas without characters. Mitchell's criticism is a more sophisticated updating of Vance Palmer's openly misogynist interpretation of why Stead fails to achieve greatness in his eyes. He sees the problem as 'a conflict in her writing between her feminine emotionality, "her natural emotional surge", and her intellect. "It is an old conflict with novelists – particularly women writers"', he adds.[17]

Critics trained in an English tradition tend to feel most offended by Stead's hybrid novels, with their defiance of decorum, while Americans are more likely to praise what they call her 'excess'. I have argued that Stead's imagination is not undisciplined, as it appears to readers looking for conventional means of organising experience, but rather highly disciplined in its search for exactly the right fictional form to convey the complexities of social relations. Constantly aware of what Teresa Hawkins terms 'the tyranny of what is written, to rack and convert',[18] Stead writes against that tyranny to free the imagination to see the world freshly.

Whether a critic sees her vision as essentially positive, with Michael Wilding, or as essentially negative, with Adrian Mitchell, seems to depend much more on the expectations that the individual critic brings to fiction than on gender. Yet gender still plays a role. Surely only a male critic could argue, as Mitchell does, that Catherine Baguenault's 'circumstances, though restrictive, are not as difficult as Stead would have it. They become oppressive by her determination to resist them' (p. 137). If only such uppity women stopped resisting their oppression, they would find themselves feeling much happier about their lot. The same kind of thinking lies behind the old sexist dictum: 'If rape's inevitable, lie back and enjoy it'.

In a more appreciative essay, Douglas Stewart finds Stead's presentation of Teresa in *For Love Alone* inconsistent, arguing that 'a fully convincing Teresa would have to be genius first and woman second; this one is the reverse'.[19] Stead's novel dramatises the wholeness of a woman who refuses such separations, insisting she can both love as a woman and create as an artist at the same time, seeing both as gestures of love for life and no contradiction between them. Yet the male critic, unaccustomed to thinking of genius and woman in the same terms and making a rigid separation between artistic creativity and sexual love, cannot accept her vision of wholeness. He sees the book's vision as constituting its central flaw. In contrast, most women critics welcome Stead's depiction of Teresa's drawing and her writing as a normal part of her life. They know that Teresa's challenging of the traditional male assumption that women must choose between sexual and artistic fulfilment is potentially liberating for women – potentially, because Stead never forgets the material circumstances that limit women's freedom to choose. In redefining woman as hero in this novel, Stead also redefines the modern artist – as someone immersed in life, not separate from it. Such a system is democratic rather than hierarchically oriented.

The problems of Stead's critical reception and of determining her place in literary traditions, then, cannot be solved by reference to gender bias alone. To deny this element, however, would be to obscure the issues further. This study has tried to show how a feminist analysis can help clarify some of the questions raised by Stead's fiction. Questions about value: value to whom and for what reasons? How are gender and class written into literary structures and how might the powerless write themselves free? Questions about power: who has it and who doesn't? How can it be shifted? How may the writer use her power? Questions about form: must a text be linear and hierarchical in structure? What are the political implications of open-endedness or of a text that constantly interrupts itself?

Stead's art will always seem more valuable to those who see art as a form of engagement with life than to those who see art as a self-contained aesthetic structure. The pleasures that come from reading Stead derive from recognition, not invention. In her world, truth is not beauty. She shows us familiar worlds defamiliarised by a presentation that defines character as a matrix of individual, political and cultural forces while insisting on the responsibility of the individual for his or her own life. Stead's a-centred plots force egalitarian readings in which the web arouses more interest than the spider. There are no heroes or villains – only traps for the unwary. Her rambling structures, generously detailed style and heavy reliance on dialogue reveal complicities hidden by tidier narrative structures. While her novels may seem anti-climactic and unfocused to the critic who expects fiction to present a conventionally ordered view of the world, they provide alternatives to the critic who seeks new ways of imagining order. The great wild hops vine in *The People with the Dogs* provides the best analogy for describing the structure of a Stead novel: pulling everything within reach into its orbit, it does not distinguish between roots and branch; it has no clear beginning nor ending; it is an interdependent system in which the man-made and the natural coexist.

Stead writes out of puzzlement with what she sees. All her books ask the same question, put a thousand different ways in as many different situations: Why do we put up with the way things are? She never pretends to know the answers. Indeed, it is because she genuinely does not know that her fiction remains so compelling in its questioning. As her narrator says of the central incident in 'The Old School': 'I was there. I was never able to make up my mind about things; and so it is still there, clear to me, the ever burning question of good and bad . . . .'[20] Stead's fiction shows us this ever burning question in a new light, the light of her own intense wish to understand and her belief that understanding can only come through attention to specific political contexts. Impatient with platitudes and conventional formulas of explanation, she created new fictional structures to house the proliferating networks of interrelations her pursuit of this question unearthed. Vast tapestries of interweaving threads, these novels make us rethink our notions of design.

Christina Stead, the writer who composed them, resists easy definition in the same way they do. She avoided other writers, preferring the company of businessmen and fellow travellers on the Left. She seems to have rebuffed Nettie Palmer's attempts to include her in Australian expatriate literary circles and her wandering lifestyle prevented the development of close links with any particular group. Stead valued her friends – most of her books are dedicated to them – but these were not usually literary friendships. As a writer, Stead was a loner.

Her work is too complex to be completely defined by any single pattern, even one as open-ended as her own adaptation of the voyage to Cythera. This metaphor has the advantage, however, of crossing the boundaries traditionally drawn between love and work and between public and private lives. It reminds us that Stead was a political writer who wrote out of a dissatisfaction as well as a fascination with the way things are. It enabled Stead to redefine love as a creative act and one that separated the sell outs from those committed to living with integrity. Through this metaphor, Stead's fiction invites her readers to question what many have seen as inevitable: traditional patterns of gender and class relations and the aesthetic values they support.

Notes

Notes to Chapter 1

1. Christina Stead, 'A Writer's Friends', *Southerly*, vol. 28, no. 3 (1968), p. 163. For the biographical information that follows, I rely on Stead's articles and interviews, on John Beston, 'A Brief Biography of Christina Stead', *World Literature Written in English*, vol. 15, no. 1 (1976), pp. 79–86 and R. G. Geering, *Christina Stead* (Twayne; rev edn Sydney: Angus & Robertson, 1979).

2. Joan Lidoff, 'An Interview with Christina Stead', *Christina Stead* (New York, Ungar, 1982), p. 202.

3. Christina Stead, 'A Waker and Dreamer', *Overland*, no. 53 (Spring 1972), pp. 33–37.

4. Joan Lidoff, op. cit., p. 209.

5. 'Christina Stead interviewed by Giulia Giuffre', *Stand*, vol. 23, no. 4 (1982), p. 25.

6. John Beston, 'An Interview with Christina Stead', *World Literature Written in English*, vol. 15, no. 1 (April 1976), p. 93.

7. Rodney Wetherall, 'Christina Stead: An Interview', *Overland*, no. 93 (1983), p. 27.

8. A. W. Barker, *Dear Robertson: Letters to an Australian Publisher* (Sydney, Angus & Robertson, 1982), pp. 137–38.

9. William Blake, *Elements of Marxian Economic Theory and its Criticism: An American Looks at Karl Marx* (New York, Cordon, 1939), p. vi.

10. *Left Review*, vol. 1, no. 11 (1935), p. 453.

11. See Christina Stead, 'Ocean of Story', *Australian Literary Studies*, vol. 10, no. 2 (1981), pp. 181–85 (reprinted from the *Kenyon Review*, vol. 30, no. 4 [1968]). For the fragment see Stead, Christina. Papers. Manuscript Collection, National Library of Australia. Ms 4967, Box 6, Folder 39. See the Prologue to *For Love Alone* (London: Virago, 1978) and pp. 192–93, 222, 238 and 348 for its Ulyssean references.

12. Rodney Wetherall, op. cit., p. 21.

13. Ann Whitehead, 'Christina Stead: An Interview', *Australian Literary Studies*, vol. 6, no. 3 (1974), p. 230.

14. John Beston, op. cit., p. 90.

15. 'What Goal in Mind?: Two Societies' in *We took their orders and are dead: an Anti-War Anthology*, eds Shirley Cass et al (Sydney, Ure Smith,

1971), pp. 119–30. For a fuller discussion of her politics, see Michael Wilding, 'Christina Stead', *Australian Literary Studies*, vol. 11, no. 2 (1983), pp. 150–51.

16. Phyllis Rose, *Parallel Lives* (New York, Vintage, 1984), pp. 6–9.

17. Joan Lidoff, op. cit., p. 219.

Notes to Chapter 2

1. R. G. Geering, *Christina Stead: A Critical Study* rev. ed. (Twayne, 1969, Sydney, Angus & Robertson, 1979); Joan Lidoff, *Christina Stead* (New York, Ungar, 1982).

2. Elaine Showalter, 'Towards a Feminist Poetics', *Women Writing and Writing About Women*, ed. Mary Jacobus (London, Croom Helm, 1979), p. 36.

3. Stead, Christina. Papers. Manuscript Collection, National Library of Australia. Ms 4967, Box 7, Folder 53.

4. Sandra M. Gilbert and Susan Gubar, *The Madwoman in the Attic: The Woman Writer and the Nineteenth-Century Imagination* (New Haven and London, Yale University Press, 1979), p. 17.

5. Ibid., p. xi.

6. Joan Lidoff, op. cit., p. 124.

7. Christina Stead, *Seven Poor Men of Sydney* (Sydney, Angus & Robertson, 1965), p. 242.

8. Don Anderson, 'Christina Stead's Unforgettable Dinner Parties', *Southerly*, vol. 39, no. 1 (March 1979), p. 31.

9. Rodney Wetherall, 'Christina Stead: An Interview', *Overland*, no. 93 (1983), p. 28.

10. Joan Lidoff, op. cit., p. 185.

11. Jonah Raskin, 'Christina Stead in Washington Square', *London Magazine*, N.S. vol. 9, no. 11 (1970), pp. 75 and 77.

12. Christina Stead, *For Love Alone* (London, Virago, 1978), pp. 192–93. Although Stead consistently spells Cythera as Cytherea, I adopt the former spelling when not quoting her. For a fuller discussion of the sources of this motif see Ian Reid, '"The Woman Problem" in Some Australian and New Zealand Novels', *Southern Review* (Adelaide), vol. 11, no. 3 (1974), pp. 187–204 and R. G. Geering, *Christina Stead*, pp. 112 and 115.

13. Terry Sturm, 'Christina Stead's New Realism', in *Cunning Exiles: Studies of Modern Prose Writers*, eds Don Anderson and Stephen Knight (Sydney, Angus & Robertson, 1974), p. 13.

Notes to Chapter 3

1. Christina Stead, *Seven Poor Men of Sydney* (Sydney, Angus & Robertson, 1965), p. 2. Hereafter cited by page.

2. Rodney Wetherall, 'Christina Stead: An Interview' *Overland*, no. 93 (1983), p. 20.

3. Christina Stead, *The Salzburg Tales* (Melbourne, Sun Books, 1966), p. 314. Hereafter cited by page.

Notes to Chapter 4

1. Christina Stead, *The Beauties and Furies* (London, Virago, 1982), p. 21. Hereafter cited by page.

2. Christina Stead, *House of All Nations* (London and Sydney, Angus & Robertson, 1974), p. 80. Hereafter cited by page.

3. Stead, Christina. Papers. Manuscript Collection, National Library of Australia. Ms 4967, Box 1, Folder 4, Fragment labelled Chapter VII, 'Change of Heart', p. 216.

Notes to Chapter 5

1. Christina Stead, *The Man Who Loved Children* (Harmondsworth, Penguin, 1970), p. 523. Hereafter cited by page.

2. Juliet Mitchell, *Woman's Estate* (Harmondsworth, Penguin, 1971), p. 99.

3. Randall Jarrell, 'An Unread Book', Introduction to *The Man Who Loved Children* cited above, p. 29.

4. Sandra M. Gilbert and Susan Gubar, *The Madwoman in the Attic* (New Haven and London, Yale University Press, 1979), pp. 54–57.

5. Christina Stead, *For Love Alone* (London, Virago, 1978), pp. 192–193. Hereafter cited by page.

6. For a fuller analysis of the influence of *Vision* on Stead's work see Ian Reid, '"The Woman Problem" in Some Australian and New Zealand Novels,' *Southern Review* (Adelaide), vol. 11, no. 3 (1974), pp. 187–204.

7. 'Christina Stead interviewed by Giulia Giuffre', *Stand*, vol. 23, no. 4 (1982), p. 24.

8. Christina Stead, 'A Harmless Affair', *Southerly* 'Christina Stead: Special Issue', Unpublished Writings, ed. R. G. Geering, vol. 44, no. 1 (March 1984), pp. 66–84.

Notes to Chapter 6

1. Christina Stead, *Letty Fox: Her Luck* (London, Virago, 1978), p. 454. Hereafter cited by page.

2. Meaghan Morris, 'Introduction', Christina Stead, *Letty Fox: Her Luck* (Sydney, Angus & Robertson, 1974).

3. Christina Stead, *A Little Tea, a Little Chat* (London, Virago, 1981), p. 17. Hereafter cited by page.

4. Christina Stead, *The People with the Dogs* (London, Virago, 1981), p. 87. Hereafter cited by page.

5. Christina Stead, *A Little Tea, a Little Chat*, op. cit., p. 4.

6. Christina Stead, 'The Puzzleheaded Girl', *The Puzzleheaded Girl* (London, Virago, 1984), p. 18. Hereafter cited by page.

7. Joan Lidoff, *Christina Stead* (New York, Ungar, 1982), p. 215.

8. Quoted in Sandra M. Gilbert and Susan Gubar, *The Madwoman in the Attic* (New Haven and London, Yale University Press, 1979), pp. 56–57.

Notes to Chapter 7

1. Sheila Rowbotham, *Woman's Consciousness, Man's World* (Harmondsworth, Penguin, 1973), p. 27.

2. Christina Stead, *Cotters' England* (London, Virago, 1980), p. 216. Hereafter cited by page.

3. Terry Sturm, 'Afterword', Christina Stead, *Cotters' England* (Sydney, Angus & Robertson, 1974), p. 353.

4. Christina Stead, *The Little Hotel* (London and Sydney, Angus & Robertson, 1973), p. 127. Hereafter cited by page.

5. Patricia Meyer Spacks, 'In Praise of Gossip', *Hudson Review* no. 35, (1982), pp. 19–38 and *Gossip* (New York, Knopf, 1985).

6. Christina Stead, *Miss Herbert (The Suburban Wife)* (London, Virago, 1982), p. 308. Hereafter cited by page.

Notes to Chapter 8

1. Elizabeth Hardwick, *A View of My Own: Essays in Literature and Society* (New York, Farrer, Strauss & Cudahy, 1962), pp. 41–48.

2. Christina Stead, 'A Writer's Friends', *Southerly*, vol. 28, no. 3 (1968), p. 164.

3. Anne Summers, 'The Self Denied: Australian Women Writers – Their Image of Women', *Refractory Girl*, vol. 2, nos 9–10 (Autumn 1973), p. 10.

4. For example, in a review of *The Man Who Loved Children*, Mary McGrory complained that 'All is distorted, turgid and overblown in her [Letty Fox's] world, with sex rampant and passion unbridled' ('Framing Father', *New Republic*, vol. 104, no. 61, 13 January 1941). Diana Trilling criticised Teresa in *For Love Alone* for seeking power not love in her review 'Women in Love', *Nation*, 28 October 1944, pp. 535–36. Marjorie Farber found the same book 'an egotistical romantic fantasy' in 'Amor, Amor, Amor', *New Republic*, 13 November 1944, p. 633. Joan Lidoff discusses these negative reviews in *Christina Stead*, pp. 99–106. Don Anderson's article, 'Christina Stead's Unforgettable Dinner Parties' (*Southerly*, vol. 39, no. 1 [1979], p. 36) takes issue with Anne Duchêne's statement that '"a sense of structure" is not one of Miss Stead's "principal gifts"' (*Times Literary Supplement*, 8 September 1978, p. 985) to argue on the contrary 'the possibility of a chaotic form (cf. Faulkner)' that *contains* without denying chaos.

5. Details in a letter to the author from Professor Geering, 30 September 1985. Other male critics who have published sensitive responses to her work are Don Anderson, Laurie Clancy, Brian Kiernan, Ian Reid, Terry Sturm and Michael Wilding.

6. *Partisan Review*, vol. XLVI, no. 2 (1979), p. 273.

7. Robert Boyers, 'The Family Novel', *Salmagundi* no. 26, (Spring 1974).

8. Joan Lidoff, 'Home is Where the Heart is: The Fiction of Christina Stead', *Southerly*, vol. 38, no. 4 (1978), p. 363.

9. Kerryn Goldsworthy, 'Interview with Angela Carter', *Meanjin*, vol. 44, no. 1 (1985), p. 6.

10. Terry Sturm, 'Christina Stead's New Realism' in *Cunning Exiles: Studies of Modern Prose Writers*, eds Don Anderson and Stephen Knight (Sydney, Angus & Robertson, 1974), p. 13.

11. Susan Higgins, 'Christina Stead's *For Love Alone*: A Female Odyssey?', *Southerly*, vol. 38, no. 4 (1978), p. 430.

12. Christina Stead, *Letty Fox: Her Luck*, op. cit., p. 383.

13. Joan Lidoff, *Christina Stead* (New York, Ungar, 1982), p. 109.

14. Margaret Harris, 'Writer and Reader', *Southerly*, vol. 44, no. 2 (1984), pp. 234–35.

15. Stead, Christina. Papers. Manuscript Collection, National Library of Australia, Ms 4967, Box 2, Folder 7.

16. Adrian Mitchell, 'Fiction', *The Oxford History of Australian Literature*, ed. Leonie Kramer (Melbourne, Oxford University Press, 1981), p. 138. Hereafter cited by page.

17. Vance Palmer, 'Australian Writers Abroad', *The Bulletin*, 10 February 1937, p. 2, quoted in John Docker, *Australian Cultural Elites: Intellectual Traditions in Sydney and Melbourne* (Sydney, Angus & Robertson, 1974), p. 96.

18. Christina Stead, *For Love Alone*, op. cit., p. 420.

19. Douglas Stewart, 'Glory and Catastrophe', *The Flesh and the Spirit* (Sydney, Angus & Robertson, 1948), p. 238.

20. Christina Stead, 'The Old School', *Southerly*, vol. 44, no. 1 (1984), p. 15.

Bibliography

For a bibliography to 1980 see, Marianne Ehrhardt, 'Christina Stead: A Checklist', *Australian Literary Studies*, vol. 9, no. 4 (1980), pp. 508–35. My list here concentrates on the period since then.

Primary Sources

Works by Christina Stead

Fiction

The Salzburg Tales (London, Peter Davies, 1934; New York, D. Appleton-Century, 1934; Melbourne, Sun, 1966).

Seven Poor Men of Sydney (London, Peter Davies, 1934; New York, D. Appleton-Century, 1934; Sydney, Angus & Robertson, 1965).

The Beauties and Furies (London, Peter Davies, 1936; New York, D. Appleton-Century, 1936; London, Virago, 1982).

House of All Nations (New York, Simon & Schuster, 1938; London, Peter Davies, 1938; Sydney, Angus & Robertson, 1974).

The Man Who Loved Children (New York, Simon & Schuster, 1940; London, Peter Davies, 1941; Harmondsworth, Penguin, 1970).

For Love Alone (New York, Harcourt, Brace, 1944; London, Peter Davies, 1945; London, Virago, 1978).

Letty Fox: Her Luck (New York, Harcourt, Brace, 1946; London, Peter Davies, 1947; London, Virago, 1978).

A Little Tea, a Little Chat (New York, Harcourt, Brace, 1948; London, Virago, 1981).

The People with the Dogs (Boston, Little, Brown, 1952; London, Virago, 1981).

Dark Places of the Heart (New York, Holt, Rinehart and Winston, 1966).

(Cotters' England) (London, Secker and Warburg, 1967; London, Virago, 1980).

The Puzzleheaded Girl (New York, Holt, Rinehart and Winston, 1967; London, Virago, 1984).

The Little Hotel (London, Sydney, Angus and Robertson, 1973; New York, Holt, Rinehart and Winston, 1975).

Miss Herbert (The Suburban Wife) (New York, Random House, 1976; London, Virago, 1982).

Articles

'The Writers Take Sides', *Left Review*, vol. 1, no. 2 (1935), pp. 453–62.

'A Writer's Friends', *Southerly*, vol. 28, no. 3 (1968), pp. 163–68.

'The International Symposium on the Short Story', Christina Stead (England), *Kenyon Review*, vol. 30, no. 4 (1968), pp. 444–50, reprinted as 'Ocean of Story', *Australian Literary Studies*, vol. 10, no. 2 (1981), pp. 181–85.

'About Woman's Insight, There is a Sort of Folklore We Inherit' *Vogue* (America), 15 September 1971, pp. 61 and 130.

'What Goal in Mind?' in *We Took Their Orders and are Dead*, eds Shirley Cass et al. (Sydney, Ure Smith, 1971), pp. 119–30.

'A Waker and Dreamer', *Overland* no. *53* (Spring 1972), pp. 33–37.

Posthumous publications

Christina Stead: Special Issue. Unpublished Writings, ed. R. G. Geering, *Southerly*, vol. 44, no. 1 (1984).

'Accents/Neighbours on the Green', *Southerly*, vol. 44, no. 2 (1984), pp. 217–32.

'Life is Difficult', *Southerly*, vol. 44, no. 3 (1984), pp. 351–64.

Interviews

Beston, John B., 'An Interview with Christina Stead', *World Literature Written in English*, vol. 15, no. 1 (April 1976), pp. 87–95.

Guiffre, Giulia, 'Christina Stead', *Stand*, vol. 23, no. 4 (1982), pp. 22–29.

Lidoff, Joan, 'Christina Stead: An Interview', *Aphra*, vol. 6, nos. 3 & 4 (1976), pp. 39–64. (Reprinted in Joan Lidoff, *Christina Stead* [New York, Ungar, 1982], pp. 180–220.)

Raskin, Jonah, 'Christina Stead in Washington Square', *London Magazine*, vol. 9, no. 2 (February 1970), pp. 70–77.

Wetherall, Rodney, 'Christina Stead: An Interview', *Overland* 93, 1983, pp. 17–29.

Whitehead, Ann, 'Christina Stead: An Interview', *Australian Literary Studies*, vol. 6, no. 3 (May 1974), pp. 230–48.

Secondary Sources

Full-length studies

Clancy, Laurie, *Christina Stead's 'The Man Who Loved Children' and 'For Love Alone'* (Melbourne, Shillington House, 1981).

Geering, R. G. *Christina Stead*, Australian Writers and their Work Series (Melbourne, Oxford University Press, 1969).

Geering, R. G. *Christina Stead* (New York, Twayne, 1969). (Rev. edn Sydney, Angus and Robertson, 1979.)

Lidoff, Joan, *Christina Stead* (New York, Ungar, 1982).

Articles and parts of books devoted to Christina Stead

Anderson, Don, 'Christina Stead's Unforgettable Dinner Parties', *Southerly*, vol. 39, no. 1 (1979), pp. 28–45.

Bader, Rudolf, 'Christina Stead and the *Bildungsroman*', *World Literature Written in English*, vol. 23, no. 1 (1984), pp. 31–39.

Clancy, Laurie, 'The Economy of Love: Christina Stead's Women' in *Who is She?*, ed. Shirley Walker (St Lucia, University of Queensland Press, 1983), pp. 136–49.

Eldershaw, M. Barnard, 'Christina Stead' in *Essays in Australian Fiction* (Melbourne, Melbourne University Press, 1938), pp. 158–81.

Fagan, Robert, 'Christina Stead', *Partisan Review*, no. 46 (1979), pp. 262–70.

Gardiner, Judith Kegan, 'Christina Stead: Dark Places of the
    Heart', *North American Review*, no. 162 (1977), pp. 67–71.
Geering, R. G. 'Christina Stead in the 1960s', *Southerly*,
    vol. 28, no. 1 (1968), pp. 26–36.
—— 'What is Normal? Two Recent Novels by Christina Stead',
    Southerly, vol. 38, no. 4 (1978), pp. 462–73.
Green, Dorothy, 'Chaos, or a Dancing Star? Christina Stead's
    Seven Poor Men of Sydney', *Meanjin*, vol. 27, no. 2 (1968),
    pp. 150–61.
—— '*The Man Who Loved Children*: Storm in a Teacup' in *The
    Australian Experience: Critical Essays on Australian Novels*, ed.
    W. S. Ramson (Canberra, Australian National University
    Press, 1974), pp. 177–208.
Hardwick, Elizabeth, 'The Neglected Novels of Christina Stead',
    New Republic, 1 August (1955), pp. 17–19. (Reprinted in *A
    View of My Own*, New York, Farrer, Strauss & Cudahy, 1962,
    pp. 41–48).
Higgins, Susan, '*For Love Alone*: A Female Odyssey?', *Southerly*,
    vol. 38, no. 4 (1978), pp. 428–45.
Holmes, Bruce, 'Character and Ideology in Christina Stead's
    House of All Nations', *Southerly*, vol. 45, no. 3 (1985), pp. 266–
    279.
Kiernan, Brian, 'Christina Stead: *Seven Poor Men of Sydney* and
    For Love Alone' in *Images of Society and Nature: Seven Essays
    on Australian Novels* (Melbourne, Oxford University Press,
    1971), pp. 59–81.
Lidoff, Joan, 'Home is Where the Heart is: The Fiction of
    Christina Stead', *Southerly*, vol. 38, no. 4 (1978), pp. 363–75.
McDonell, Jennifer, 'Christina Stead's *The Man Who Loved
    Children*', *Southerly*, vol. 44, no. 4 (1984), pp. 394–413.
McGregor, Grant, '*Seven Poor Men of Sydney*: The Historical
    Dimension', *Southerly*, vol. 38, no. 4 (1978), pp. 380–404.
Perkins, Elizabeth, 'Energy and Originality in some Characters
    of Christina Stead', *Journal of Commonwealth Literature*,
    vol. 15, no. 1 (1980), pp. 107–13.
Pybus, Rodney, 'The Light and the Dark: The Fiction of
    Christina Stead', *Stand*, vol. 10, no. 1 (1968), pp. 30–37.
Reid, Ian, '"The Woman Problem" in Some Australian and New

Zealand Novels', *Southern Review* (Adelaide), vol. 7, no. 3 (1974), pp. 187–204.

Sage, Lorna, 'Inheriting the Future: *For Love Alone*', *Stand*, vol. 23, no. 4 (1982), pp. 34–39.

Sheridan, Susan, '*The Man Who Loved Children* and the Patriarchal Family Drama', in *Gender, Politics and Fiction: Twentieth Century Australian Women's Novels*, ed. Carole Ferrier (St Lucia, University of Queensland Press, 1985), pp. 136–149.

Smith, Graeme Kinross, 'Christina Stead', *Australia's Writers* (Melbourne, Nelson, 1980), pp. 209–16.

Strauss, Jennifer, 'An Unsentimental Romance: Christina Stead's *For Love Alone*', *Kunapipi*, vol. 4, no. 2 (1982), pp. 82–94.

Sturm, Terry, 'Christina Stead's New Realism' in *Cunning Exiles: Studies of Modern Prose Writers*, eds D. Anderson and S. Knight (Sydney, Angus & Robertson, 1974), pp. 9–35.

Summers, Anne, 'The Self Denied: Australian Women Writers – Their Image of Women', *Refractory Girl*, no. 2 (1973), pp. 4–11.

Tracey, Lorna, 'The Virtue of the Story: *The Salzburg Tales*', *Stand*, vol. 23, no. 4 (1982), pp. 48–53.

Wilding, Michael, 'Christina Stead's Australian Novels', *Southerly*, vol. 27, no. 1 (1967), pp. 20–33.

—— 'Christina Stead', *Australian Literary Studies*, vol. 11, no. 2 (1983), pp. 150–51.

Yglesias, Jose, 'Marx as Muse', *Nation* (New York), no. 100, pp. 363–70.

Background reading

Aaron, Daniel, *Writers on the Left* (New York, Oxford University Press, 1977).

Abel, Elizabeth (ed.), *Writing and Sexual Difference* (Chicago, University of Chicago Press, 1982).

De Beauvoir, Simone, *The Second Sex* (New York, Alfred Knopf, 1952).

Blau DuPlessis, Rachel, *Writing Beyond the Ending: Narrative Strategies of Twentieth-Century Women Writers* (Bloomington, Indiana University Press, 1985).

Eagleton, Terry, *Criticism and Ideology* (London, New Left Books, 1976).

Ferrier, Carole (ed.) *Gender, Politics and Fiction: Twentieth-Century Australian Women's Novels* (St Lucia, University of Queensland Press, 1985).

Firestone, Shulamith, *The Dialectic of Sex* (London, Cape, 1971).

Gilbert, Sandra M. and Gubar, Susan, *The Madwoman in the Attic: The Woman Writer and the Nineteenth-Century Imagination* (New Haven and London, Yale University Press, 1979).

Jacobus, Mary (ed.), *Women Writing and Writing about Women* (London, Croom Helm, 1979).

Kramer, Leonie (ed.), *The Oxford History of Australian Literature* (Melbourne, Oxford University Press, 1981).

Lukács, Georg, *The Historical Novel*, trans. Hannah and Stanley Mitchell (Harmondsworth, Penguin, 1981).

Macherey, Pierre, *A Theory of Literary Production*, trans. G. Wall (London, Routledge & Kegan Paul, 1978).

Mitchell, Juliet, *Woman's Estate* (Harmondsworth, Penguin, 1971).

Rose, Phyllis, *Parallel Lives: Five Victorian Marriages* (New York, Vintage, 1984).

Rowbotham, Sheila, *Woman's Consciousness, Man's World* (Harmondsworth, Penguin, 1973).

Showalter, Elaine (ed.), *The New Feminist Criticism: Essays on Women, Literature and Theory* (New York, Pantheon, 1985).

Walker, Shirley (ed.), *Who is She? Images of Women in Australian Fiction* (St Lucia, University of Queensland Press, 1983).

Index

Anderson, Don 24
Austen, Jane 150
Australian literary context 2, 5, 7, 13, 46, 80, 161

Balzac, Honoré de 6, 12, 21, 164
Blake, William (Stead's husband) 5, 8–9, 12, 15, 23, 118, 127, 162
Blau Du Plessis, Rachel 29
Bloom, Harold 162

Carter, Angela 54, 164
Communism 113, 145; see also Marx

Darwin, Charles 7, 25, 27, 140
De Beauvoir, Simone 39

Eliot, George 33

Faust 167
Feminism 3, 13, 16–19, 29, 39–41, 54–5, 72–6, 87–8, 93–4, 96–8, 116–18, 147–9, 152, 155, 163, 171; see also Gender and Misogyny
Freud, Sigmund 26, 73, 76, 100, 168–9

Geering, R. G. 16, 162–3, 165
Gender 3, 4, 14, 15, 20, 72, 86, 91, 161–2, 171; see also Feminism and Misogyny

Gilbert, Sandra M. and Gubar, Susan 21, 76, 121
Gothic 21–2
Green, Dorothy 163

Hardwick, Elizabeth 160
Harris, Margaret 166

Ideology 17, 85, 100–101, 125–6, 134, 154, 158, 165

Jarrell, Randall 73–4
Joyce, James
Portrait of the Artist as a Young Man 70
Ulysses 57

Lawrence, D. H. 33, 168
Leavis, F. R. 36, 156, 159
Lidoff, Joan 16, 22–3, 106, 163–4, 165–6
Lindsay, Jack 80–1
Lukacs, Georg 159

Marx, Karl 4, 9, 27, 34, 107, 133, 136, 141, 158, 164; see also Communism
Misogyny 38, 45–6, 54, 62–5, 103–104; see also Feminism and Gender
Mitchell, Adrian 161–2, 169, 170
Mitchell, Juliet 18, 73
Morris, Meaghan 91

Nietzsche, Friedrich 20, 27, 79, 164

Rhys, Jean 10, 168
Rose, Phyllis 15
Rowbotham, Sheila 128

Shelley, Percy Bysshe 4, 6,
 70, 71, 77
Sheridan, Susan 165
Showalter, Elaine 18
Socialism 13, 14, 18–19,
 66–7, 113, 122–3, 162,
 165–6
'The Sons of Clovis' 2, 41–2
Spacks, Patricia Meyer 141
Stead, Christina
 fairy-tale motifs in her
  fiction:
  Sleeping Beauty 51
  Snow White 75–6, 121
  The Ugly Duckling 70
 imagery:
  of dinner parties 132–3,
   144–5, 153
  of the hall of mirrors 41–
   2, 57, 127–8, 131,
   135, 143
  of waking and dreaming
   4, 41, 56–7, 70, 87,
   117, 123, 151
 her publications:
  A Little Tea, a Little Chat
   12, 25, 29, 96, 101–
   107, 108, 112, 143,
   168
  Cotters' England (Dark
   Places of the Heart)
   12, 30, 128–38, 143,
   145, 157, 158, 162
  For Love Alone 8, 10, 11,
   22, 27, 55, 57, 80–9,
   90, 108, 110, 157–8,
   160, 162, 170–1
  I'm Dying Laughing 163

Letty Fox: Her Luck 12,
  17, 22, 29, 90–101,
  108, 152, 167
Miss Herbert (The
  Suburban Wife) 13,
  24, 55, 145–58
'Ocean of Story' 10
'The Old School' 6,
  172
Seven Poor Men of
  Sydney 9, 23–4, 29,
  32–43, 44, 46, 76,
  127, 160, 164, 167
'The Writers Take
  Sides' 9
The Beauties and Furies
  10, 23, 48–57, 84,
  168
The House of All Nations
  10–11, 25, 29, 30, 50,
  52, 53, 58–68, 69,
  101, 103, 105–106
The Little Hotel 13, 138–
  45
The Man Who Loved
  Children 6, 11, 17,
  27, 69–79, 80, 81, 90,
  108, 138, 156, 160,
  162, 163
The People With the Dogs
  12, 25, 29, 96, 107–
  15, 135, 172
The Puzzleheaded Girl
  12, 115
'The Dianas' 120–1,
  125–6
'The Girl From the
  Beach' 121–3,
  125–6
'The Right-Angled
  Creek' 123–6
'The Puzzleheaded
  Girl' 116–20, 125–6

Stead, Christina – *continued*
  her publications – *continued*
    The Salzburg Tales 9, 44–
        7, 160
      'The Gold Bride' 44
      'Marionettist' 44
      'Overcote' 44
      'The Triskelion' 76
Stead, David 4, 5–8
Stead, Ellen 5
Stewart, Douglas 170
Sturm, Terry 30, 129, 164,
    165

Summers, Anne 161

Vision 80–1

Watteau, *The Embarkation for
    Cythera*
  imagery of Venus 52–3, 151
  imagery of the voyage 2,
      15, 27, 49, 57, 80, 89,
      101, 151, 159, 173
Wilding, Michael 170
Woolf, Virginia 19, 92, 167,
    168